Creating
Partnerships

Previous publications by Cynthia King:

"Creating Partnership Organizations," in the
UNESCO Encyclopedia of Life Support Systems
(EOLSS), 2004.

"Wildland Recreation and Intercultural
Communication" (audio recording), 1990.

Creating Partnerships

Unleashing Collaborative Power
in the Workplace

Cynthia King, PhD

Wisdom Way Press

Santa Barbara, California

Excerpts of the present work, in a slightly different version, were previously published, © 2004 Eolss Publishers Co., Ltd. ("Creating Partnership Organizations," by Cynthia King, PhD, in the UNESCO *Encyclopedia of Life Support Systems*, with permission from Eolss Publishers Co., Ltd.)

"Stubborn Ounces (To One Who Doubts the Worth of Doing Anything If You Can't Do Everything)," from HANDS LAID UPON THE WIND by Bonaro W. Overstreet. Copyright © 1955 by W.W. Norton & Co. Inc. Used by permission of W.W. Norton & Company, Inc.

Published by Wisdom Way Press, P.O. Box 8913, Santa Barbara, CA 93118. For ordering information, go to www.thewisdomway.com.
Printed in the United States of America on acid-free recycled paper by Central Plains Book Manufacturing
Cover design by Dotti Albertine, Albertine Book Design

Publisher's Cataloging-in-Publication
(Provided by Quality Books, Inc.)

King, Cynthia, 1949-
    Creating partnerships : unleashing collaborative
    power in the workplace / Cynthia King.
    p. cm.
    Includes bibliographical references and index.
    LCCN 2005902260
    ISBN 0-9766377-0-7

    1. Teams in the workplace--Management.
    2. Organizational effectiveness. 3. Communication in
    organizations.   I. Title.

HD66.K557 2005   658.4'022
                        QBI05-200102

To the courageous, creative, and dedicated
individuals of the NEFA organization.

You have my respect for your willingness to enter
the wilderness of organizational transition,
and gratitude for your inspiring example of
partnering leadership.

☙ Contents ❧

❧ Preface ❧

Creating Partnerships is at its heart a book about peacemaking. Peace begins with each individual and grows within the fertile soil of our relationships with each other. Organizations of all types—whether corporations or community groups, public agencies or religious or educational institutions—provide the context for many of our most consuming and productive relationships, and therefore act as a crucible for learning to manage difficult situations and conflicts. For that reason, the organizational context, which resides within the matrices of both individual and global relationships, provides the focus of this work.

In the rapidly changing social, economic, and political milieu of the early twenty-first century, the vast majority of organizations rely on a predominant operating system that is based on separation, discrimination that leads to prejudice, and the use of *power-over* methods to achieve domination and control. That system is the patriarchy, which has been evolving and becoming ever more entrenched for thousands of years. At its root, the patriarchal system is based on personal egoism and narcissism, even when the organization is "ruled" by a benevolent autocracy rather than a stern dictatorship. In that system, many people trust that the solution to organizational difficulties and economic disparities is to find a "better patriarch"—a strong leader who will force things to improve. The patriarchal system has informed core management practices for the majority of traditional business, educational, social welfare, and community organizations for so long that most people are hard pressed to imagine another way of operating.

Nevertheless, there is growing recognition that in order to develop sustainable societies, the organizations that run those societies must develop operating principles that support human dignity, peaceful interactions, and both economic and environmental viability. Rather than maintaining and rewarding loyalty to the hierarchical *power-over* system of competition and tight controls, there is a choice to engage in partnerships that represent loyalty to service and an expansiveness that unleashes talent, innovation, and creativity.

A different sort of integrity springs from that context; rather than relying on principles of self-preservation and individualistic "success," or settling for token participation in organizational processes, we move to partnership principles, wherein we recognize that we are simultaneously independent and *inter*dependent. Thus, *Creating Partnerships* offers a model that (1) fosters peaceful solutions to conflicting power struggles within organizations, and (2) builds leadership capacity for all organizational partner-members. Both elements contribute to changing organizational culture, and in turn strengthening sustainable partnerships.

I felt compelled to write this book after working with a wide variety of organizations over the past 25 years, both as a program manager and Executive Director, and then as an independent organizational consultant. During that time, I observed a variety of approaches to organizing business, educational, nonprofit, and community groups, and I encountered many situations that were frustrating for both my clients and me. I experienced and shared the frustration of many organizational members who were saddled with bosses who talked the talk of teamwork and partnership, but then proceeded to define team loyalty as playing by *their* rules and placing priority on *their* point of view. In these situations, managers asked why their employees refused to "get with the program." This mindset disregards the frustration of individuals who have had their hopes raised with team talk only to be co-opted when they realized that this "talk" was simply "window dressing," or another veil of false promises. Furthermore, this kind of treatment is manipulative and breeds the cynicism that erodes morale and productivity.

I also experienced—to varying degrees, in a number of settings—the rigors of transforming a traditional top-down hierarchy into a collaborative partnership. In this process I witnessed the deep meaning, satisfaction, and enhanced productivity that is derived when an organization achieves a truly shared partnership. Throughout these years of working within organizations, I have come to realize that there are very few people who understand at the everyday level—where individuals struggle with nitty-gritty details and interpersonal rapport—how true partnership is qualitatively different from our traditional system. Indeed, partnership represents a significant departure from our taken-for-granted version of power dynamics, leadership, and relationships within the organization, as well as between the organization and its stakeholders and customers.

Creating Partnerships was written to address the need for a different way of perceiving relationships and operating in organizational arenas. This is neither a management treatise about how to control others to get the most out of them, nor a political perspective about how to manipulate the system for maximum gain. Rather, *Creating Partnerships* offers a different philosophy and method of organizational communication. It first examines how people share their passions and co-create a common vision, and second, builds on the ground of relationship and demonstrates how to collaborate in ways that are flexible and innovative, and simultaneously productive and efficient. These combined elements ultimately improve organizational effectiveness and profitability.

Creating Partnerships presents a fresh approach to problems exacerbated by the outmoded system that depends on separation, top-down hierarchies, domination and control.

This traditional paradigm—the patriarchal *system, not* individual "bad men"—is further fueled by competition and partisanship, and maintained by enforcing power *over* other individuals and groups. Clearly, a stream of powerful patriarchs, who have been both male and female, has steadily reinforced the patriarchal system over the past five thousand years. While "patriarch" originally connoted the father of a household, within the patriarchal *system* it has come to represent egotistical, narcissistic, and dominating behavior by individuals (or groups) of either gender. Therein lies the crux of the organizational paradigm shift that partnership represents: Individuals move away from rampant individualism and rank-based competition where the winner-takes-all, and into shared responsibility and credit, where "we" is at least equal to "me." This represents a major cultural shift for many individuals and organizations.

The *Partnership Model* involves essentially reframing how power is managed and how leadership is manifested within organizations. This is a method for healing deep divisions and transforming our organizations, those institutions where people spend significant shares of their days and ultimately their lives. Although it is possible to find examples of successful partnerships operating within business, government, educational, or nonprofit communities, the *Partnership Model* is far from the norm in a command-and-control world. Moving from a patriarchal system to partnership admittedly represents a journey into largely uncharted territory for an American society that is historically reared on competition and exploitation of human, natural, and cultural resources. Nevertheless, we will examine numerous examples of successful partnerships.

Creating Partnerships offers both a vision and a process for achieving an effective model for our organizations as they operate within a world that is ever more complex, more globally interdependent, and more rapidly changing. The vision is one that supports a strong, productive work ethic while weaving a supporting fabric of dignity based on dialogue, mutual respect, conscious efforts to build trust, and shared progress. The *Partnership Model* is capable of responding to rapidly shifting needs, data, priorities, and interdependencies. It also advances the concept of *true progress* by moving beyond the materialistic paradigm of "growth at all costs," led by autocratic heroes and both male and female patriarchs with vested interests in maintaining status quo hierarchies. The *Partnership Model* invites conversation, participation, flexible systems, and soulful enterprise from everyone in the organization as it navigates its way through intricate global system dynamics.

If you are someone who adheres to the religion of certitude, which is based on the belief that the manager or "leader" is always right, or at least can admit no mistakes, and you support the practice of maintaining strict control of the "troops"—then be forewarned: *Creating Partnerships* will challenge many basic assumptions and core beliefs. If, on the other hand, you have an inkling or a hope that things could operate differently—that organizations, community groups, and governing bodies could build something that is truly a partnership, where the sum of the parts is synergistically greater than the whole, where everyone's voice is heard, and where the fundamental belief system is built on mutual respect and trust—then you will find here a map for the journey involved in making the transition from the traditional operational system to an entirely new model.

This book provides a map of the partnership territory. It is not the detailed set of instructions you would expect at a car rally, with a definable, predictable outcome. Rather, it is a map that describes the "lay of the land" and the characteristics of the desired outcome, and warns of pitfalls where well-meaning partnership initiatives can be caught or co-opted by those who believe in or benefit from maintaining the status quo. In keeping with the multi-level nature of the systemic change it promotes, this book can be accessed through various levels: the examples and stories of individuals and organizations where partnership is flourishing; the myths, or shared stories, that provide both historical and cultural insights; and the careful recognition of the patriarchal system and examination of the juxtaposed *Partnership Model*. Although each of these levels contributes to understanding the partnership territory, no doubt there will be particular elements that are especially timely for each reader who is embarking on their own path to partnership.

The opening chapter, "Unpacking the Patriarchy," examines the underlying system that generates the structure and operation of most organizations in American society. As previously mentioned, this is the *system* based on domination and control, and does *not* refer only to fathers or even only to men. It recognizes that many men have also been caught in the machinations of a system based on unending competition, stereotypes, and "winner takes all," and that some of the most difficult patriarchs are women.

Chapter 2, "Awakening the Potential of Partnership," explores the *Partnership Model* as applied to organizational settings, including the characteristics of a partnership organization (how would you know one if you saw it?), and the high-level strategies for making the shift.

Chapter 3, "The Paradox of Power in the Partnership Organization," explores different ways of holding and expressing power: *power-over* versus *power-with* or *power-from-within*. It also reframes the dynamic between power and conflict within the partnership paradigm such that conflicts can be transformed at the relationship level. In that respect, Dr. Marc Porter presents a valuable model for transforming relationships and conflicts, and understanding their dynamics within a partnership organization, in a special section on "Powerful Partnerships in the Common Ground."

Chapter 4, "Leadership in a Partnership Context," delves into the fundamental differences between traditional management practices and the practice of soulful leadership. Within that paradigm, service and stewardship are essential, and mentoring is seen as a process of midwifing, wherein the mentor guides and supports new growth and a process of innovative discovery, rather than opportunistically pursuing another avenue for reinforcing traditional management personae. The leader is recognized as a key partner in the creation of truly partnership organizations.

Chapter 5, "Organizational Partnerships: The Living Proof," describes a variety of successful partnerships within corporate, government, non-profit, and grassroots organizational examples. An in-depth case study of a state-level organization of a federal agency is presented. This organization has an 8-year track record as a partnership enterprise, and has succeeded in spite of existing within the authoritarian, hierarchical framework of the federal bureaucracy.

Chapter 6, "Building the Partnership Community," examines a variety of partnership community models that exist in cultures both past and present. It also considers an intercultural frame of reference that includes both organizational and international partnership examples. These models provide specific tools and applications that result in higher morale and engagement, which in turn often reduce turnover and lost productivity due to illness, sabotage, or underground conflicts.

Chapter 7, "Weaving New Patterns and Changing the Story," offers insight into the transition process, as it reflects ancient initiation patterns. Special attention is given to the transitions required to shift organizational cultures, myths, and relationships. It also summarizes a vision of what is possible with a shift into partnership organizations.

It is important to remember that in the sometimes-overwhelming global context where it is easy to feel powerless and vulnerable to those in control, we are all in this together. As we recall Gandhi's exhortation that "We must *be* the change we want for the world," we also remember that it is up to each one of us to take responsibility to make a difference. The *Partnership Model* offers a place for individuals to start, with specific changes that can be made in the myriad organizations that collectively shape our society and command large portions of our time and energies. In spite of the vast power of the patriarchal system and its adherents, *Creating Partnerships* offers reason for hope. There is another model available; there are people who are committed to realizing and applying that alternative, and there are organizations showing that it can and does work.

Realizing a profound shift in the operational norms within American organizations is of the utmost importance; the time for complacency is over. Engaged partners are needed at all levels of the wide range of organizations in American society. In the wise words of Buckminster Fuller, "There are no passengers on spaceship Earth. There is only crew."

Cynthia King
Goleta, California
April 2005

✑ Chapter 1 ✐

Unpacking the Patriarchy

Why This Focus is Important at This Time

The huge drama that is now unfolding on the world stage makes anyone's particular humblings look like so much humus. (Houston, *Jump Time* 8)

In the context of complex, disruptive social conditions that challenge organizations in the early twenty-first century, there is a deep and growing need to find another way of operating. On the large scale, these challenges include massive new epidemics such as AIDS and SARS, the institutionalization of so-called "free markets" that especially benefit large corporate and agri-business interests while forcing small entrepreneurs and family farms into destitution, and on-going, proliferating wars fought over ethnic and religious conflicts and long-simmering struggles for self-determination. On the smaller, everyday scale, millions of people experience mounting frustration at workplaces where they feel used and abused, and not respected for their potential contributions. When pushed to the edge of their frustrations, some individuals resort to domestic abuse, or explode in a reaction that has come to be known in the vernacular as "going postal."

Many are resigned to those conditions, and assume "that's just the way it is." Yet there is growing awareness that American society is in need of an operating system that promotes a wider base of participation rather than relying on exclusivity; that fosters organizational partnerships rather than maintaining strict top-down hierarchies; and that sustains personal, visionary leadership committed to stewardship of resources rather than their exploitation for the benefit of a select few. In that light, we are called to create a society where circles and communities of trust flourish, where collaboration replenishes our sense of security and direction, and where integrity grows from a larger sense of service to our shared progress.

A cultural transformation is called for: not just to repair the existing crumbling infrastructure, but to replace it. Indeed, as community activist and cultural theorist Sharif Abdullah observed in *Creating a World That Works for All*, "We live in a world that works only for a few." Therefore, he declares, "Our times cry out for change" because from his perspective, "America is coming apart at the seams" (28). While a fortunate few may be content to reinforce—and exploit—the status quo, there is growing discontent fueling calls for substantive transformation of social, economic and political systems. This book outlines a compelling and proven path toward such transformation, and the fresh organizational framework offered herein seeks to replace the current system and its over-reliance on "might makes right" with a viable alternative.

I am writing about this path because I sense there is a deep yearning for an alternative to the heroic and patriarchal myths that inform our society and our organizational cultures; an alternative that both challenges and moves beyond the narrow weave of our traditional Eurocentric, and ultimately Americentric culture. I am outlining a map that integrates a wide diversity of perspectives, outlooks, and approaches within its circle. I believe it is not imperative that that context ever existed in the past, and that it is entirely possible for organizations to operate without having to rely on a previous model, although examples of partnerships within the organizational context are provided in this book. I have had opportunities to witness that within the partnership alternative there are other ways for human beings to operate and "be" on this earth, rather than perpetuating and enduring an oppressive, *power-over* existence within the historic patriarchal system based on competition, domination, and control.

The alternative I am proposing is an inclusive system of *power-with* partnership, where all voices have the right to be heard—not just the powerful voices of those in charge—and where all individuals have full membership in their communities—no matter what their gender, race, religion, age, sexuality, or abilities. This shift represents admittedly massive movement within widely held American worldviews, and yet I am not the first—and certainly won't be the last—to advocate this shift. There are many partnership advocates identifying key elements in the shift. As mythologist and United Nations consultant Jean Houston observes, this "new way of being in community" will require "movement from the egocentric and the ethnocentric to the worldcentric." Furthermore, she confirms, "Critical to this reformation is a true partnership society, in which women join men in the full social agenda" (*Jump Time* 13). Such a society invites and celebrates equally both feminine and masculine expressions of our collective humanity (both of which already co-exist within both men and women).

Throughout this work I examine and reference myths —the storylines of a culture and an organization—as a way to help explain how and why we have evolved to the current expressions of the patriarchal system. This examination is useful for understanding both what is important to keep and what must be dismantled and replaced if we are to move forward toward a system based on partnering.

I have found it possible to take threads from ancient myths and indigenous wisdom traditions, and combine them with the ideas of courageous, visionary thinkers and creative new views and thoughts, thereby standing on the shoulders of wise men and women who have pioneered the way and painted inventive and insightful images. With this combination, we can weave a new tapestry that addresses the challenges of our times—at both individual and collective levels—and that moves our collective mythology forward into a new era that honors all perspectives and makes room for all voices in the collective dialogue.

This process of examining, unpacking, elaborating, and understanding core myths reflects the kind of fundamental, systemic change that is portrayed, for example, by examining the styles and strategies of Athena, ancient Greek goddess of war and the city-state, side by side with those of Oprah, a modern American phenomenon who has created a powerful and popular platform for dialogue and reform. While Athena demonstrates partnership in her guise as Mentor in *The Odyssey*, she also provides the classic "father's daughter" role model; the woman who aligns herself with and supports the patriarchy, or "rule of the fathers." On the other hand, Oprah offers a role model, and in some instances a support system, for women and other minorities seeking to rise above the systemic circumstances that would conspire to hold them back. Furthermore, while she speaks directly to women and minorities, her message also appeals to many men whose own philosophies resonate with hers.

Working in true partnership is not a brand-new innovation; it is an idea with a track record whose time has come, and which is steadily gaining momentum. I am adding my voice, concern, and efforts to advancing this partnership movement, which has already moved out of the theoretical realm and into real-life applications. Long-time community organizer and activist Grace Lee Boggs describes striking examples of individuals who are working for a fundamental shift toward a partnership ethic in the American social system, and who realize both the enormity of the undertaking and its critical importance. Boggs cites Pamela Chiang, an

Asian-American environmental justice organizer, who asserts, "The democracy we're creating is not about winning a seat at the table but about changing the rules of the game" (59). This idea that the basic "rules," or operating systems need to be changed has been steadily growing within our culture. Boggs also endorses grassroots organizers Vincent Harding and Rosemary Harding, who worked closely with Martin Luther King, Jr. They remember that, in the last two years of his life, Dr. King "was calling for a radical revolution in values and a radical reconstruction of our society" that would make it more inclusive and just. Harding and Harding further believe, "Making a more perfect union is sacred work, requiring faith and courage" (59).

Contrary to those who label efforts to question or change the system as not being "team players," or even "unpatriotic," the Hardings conclude that based on their experiences, "The only way to protect democracy is to advance it" (59). An important benefit of the *Partnership Model* lies in its offering of a framework for all courageous lovers of egalitarian and truly democratic ideals. Thus, this book is not a surface-level attempt to change the levels of equality within the existing system, so that everyone has equal opportunity to dominate and be on top. Instead, this is a challenge to the substratum—the very system itself—that underlies thousands of years of history and the core institutions of the Eurocentric, Americentric, and androcentric (male-centered) models.

Challenging the substratum with this proposed movement from a *power-over* system to one based on *power-with* partnership represents nothing less than a cultural transformation. For those raised within the dualistic (either-or, rather than both-and), command-and-control paradigm, a truly alternative system is often difficult to imagine and comprehend. Nevertheless, I have worked with many people who do understand the need for a paradigm shift, who are uncovering the nuts and bolts actions required and committed to making the transition, and who are dedicated to working for the full integration of the Constitutional ideals of equality and justice for all. Given the core understandings of the partnership alternative and a few key tools, they can collaboratively move the myth of competition and control forward into collaboration and partnership in order to discover our collective potential, and to consciously co-create organizational partnerships and community-based solutions to solve the complex problems we face.

Together we are called to step powerfully forward into creating a new way of working together. With more awareness of organizational cultural patterns, it is becoming apparent that the old forms, which once propelled society, are corrupted from within, and a new paradigm is struggling to be born. As we labor through the transition into this partnership process, it is also important to investigate the shadow aspects of our organizations. These "shadows" represent the "dark side," or the aspects of the organization that are pushed into the background and often denied, even as they are mirrored in the individuals who make up the organization. They are the weaknesses behind the projected strengths, where the early benefits of the patriarchal system have disintegrated into rule by supremacy of power, and where a primal fear of losing control and dominance might dissuade organizational members from implementing key changes and transitions. These are also the places where we can find ourselves resorting to old patterns of exclusivity and manipulation when faced with threats and the stresses of a competitive society. Indeed, even with the best intentions of operating as true partners and teams, given that "under stress, we regress"—it is all too easy to revert back to our old habits, perspectives, and operating principles.

In the midst of polarizing debates about how best to proceed in the face of escalating global violence and eroding natural resources, we are called both individually and collectively to step away from perpetuating the current operating system. This requires fundamental changes, needed at both the societal and the individual levels. Those changes begin with individual actions. As sociology professor Allan Johnson declares in *The Gender Knot: Unraveling Our Patriarchal Legacy*, by consciously choosing alternatives in our everyday lives that do not revolve around control and oppression, "we make it easier for others to do so as well, *and harder for them not to*" (238). Furthermore, he explains, we "weaken the patriarchal paradigm by openly choosing alternative paths in our daily lives and thereby providing living anomalies that don't fit the prevailing paradigm" (239). Even though stepping out as the odd one out requires courage, Johnson contends that contrary to popular belief, "We aren't simple prisoners of a socially constructed reality," and individuals can transform the ways we live and work together. He explains, "Reality is being constructed and reconstructed all the time, and the part we play in that, however small, gives us the chance and the responsibility to choose" to make a difference (154).

Eventually, by each person choosing to make changes, the ripple effects of those changes widen, and those forms and values that were traditionally held as normal and legitimate begin to lose their sense of obvious-ness, and new forms and values "emerge to challenge their privileged place in social life" (Johnson 239). Thus, in keeping with Gandhi's exhortation: "We must *be* the change we want for the world," it is important to realize that together we can and will make a difference. The *Partnership Model* offers a place to launch our individual and collective efforts for specific changes in our organizations.

We have collectively endured several thousand years of investment in a system of domination, which draws its potency from hierarchies of competition and control. It is ever more apparent that social and economic conditions within that system most favor those who view power as vested in positions, which to varying degrees enables them to control the lives of others through material means and narrow self-interests. Those privileged with such power, as well as many stifled by that power, come to believe in the image of the "economic man," which is anyone motivated by a need to compete for scarce resources and an innate conviction that in order to guarantee survival one cannot not compete. That conviction, that competition is the only option, in itself becomes a trap. Lilly Tomlin aptly named the unfortunate fallout from this worldview, when she observed, "The trouble with the rat race is that even if you win, you're still a rat."

In that light, there is a growing need for a shift in the fundamental system that operates as the basis of American social, political, educational, religious, and economic organizations. In spite of unparalleled wealth, rising patriotic fervor, and the promises of democracy, deep cracks scar the façade of American greatness. The implications of core myths, or cultural stories that shape American culture, definitely require serious examination if we expect to emerge with viable organizing principles and leadership models in the face of increasingly complex global conundrums coupled with ever more pluralistic societies.

These issues are particularly pressing because the United States of America in the early twenty-first century is clutching its status as the single remaining "superpower." That standing carries an immense responsibility to affect future global trajectories, especially in the ways in which people organize and address common issues, make use of power, lead one another in the creation of wealth, and create a sustainable future. These conditions can be better understood by examining how certain core myths—including the myths of the hero and of the patriarchal system—have both promoted and constrained our definitions of progress.

This examination is important because we are living in a time of heightened terrorist threat and compromised civil liberties; exposed multi-billion dollar scandals of corporate greed; serial betrayals by political leaders that rock the trust of millions in and outside their home countries; relentless environmental degradation; global shifts in employment that leave one community with intractable unemployment while jobs are "outsourced" to people in another country, thereby dramatically changing the lifestyles and worldviews of that country; and over-stretched and under-funded social programs buckling from growing populations, increasing cultural complexity, and the escalating, daunting costs of human health care. Furthermore, even as access to unbiased information is rapidly shrinking due to steadily merging media outlets, the enormous impact of the Internet, which speeds global connections and requires increased flexibility, innovation, and intercultural competence, is stretching over and weaving through all of the above circumstances.

Even though the United States of America is still the richest and single most productive country in the world, that hegemony appears to be shifting. In the early twenty-first century, the rise of the European Union and China in the global market is being intensified by the decline of the dollar as the "gold standard." Meanwhile, national unemployment level statistics largely mask the harsh reality of a "jobless recovery." They do not reflect the millions of unemployed workers who have used up their benefits and are therefore no longer counted, or of "underemployment," which includes workers with higher skills barely making ends meet because they are forced in a tight job market to accept low-paying or part-time jobs that do not include access to health-care benefits, but are nonetheless counted as "employed" (Armas; James). This grim actuality is a far cry from the American

Dream we are promised in ubiquitous advertisements that punctuate our consciousness as much as they foreclose on every acre of public space. It creates a painful gap for many who dream the dream but are trapped in a harsh reality of shrinking labor opportunities and a rapidly eroding safety net. No wonder Americans feel more stressed at work, more disillusioned and divided when we go to the polls, more dissatisfied by the loss of leisure, and more prone to serious illness stimulated by stress.

The patterns of our culture are compulsive, as reflected by the host of addiction-based twelve-step groups and the cycles of attack and retaliation that seem to feed some deep, addictive urge. Whether an attack springs from avowed terrorist organizations, is gang-related, or emerges from the organizational underground of ruthless competition and sabotage, the standard reactionary impulse is to crack down harder and faster on the perceived attackers, based on the belief that "the best defense is a good offense." In that respect, the current fascination with winner-takes-all "reality shows" showcases a profound willingness to win at the expense of the losers, and both reflects and reinforces the notion that "that's just the way it is."

In the geopolitical arena, we face an uncertain future because a controversial—and widely considered unprovoked—war in the Middle East has further destabilized the region by stirring what some Muslim clerics have declared is a "holy war" against the United States. Fundamentalists on both sides—Christian and Muslim—antagonize each other with judgment, blame, and demands. As a result of those calls to the faithful, which are reinforced by on-going attacks and steadily increasing desperation, the ranks of recruits into terrorist groups bent on creating fear and chaos within both industrial powers and struggling democratic movements have swollen exponentially since the initial 2003 invasion. With the U.S. Secretary of State telling the United Nations in

2004 that the U.S. forces may remain in Iraq until 2014, and the on-going alienation and polarization of former allies, the future seems uncertain indeed.

Meanwhile, grand displays of political power give lip service to the desperate human dramas—both from natural disasters and periodic genocidal rampages—being played out on the world stage. Periodic infusions of funds and personnel do little to resolve significant underlying social problems, and more to sustain a fundamentally *power-over* and codependent worldview based on competition, domination, and control. This system has at its ideological roots Eurocentrism, which is the view that European culture provides the most valuable central operating principles for all civilized societies. Yet this view has evolved since the shift of industrial power to the U.S. after WWI, and been fertilized by "Americentrism"—a perspective in which U.S. culture is held up as the measure of all greatness in the world, whether that be political freedom, standard of living, cultural creativity, or innovation and intellectual superiority. That self-indulgent and narcissistic belief system is being confronted by groups that espouse their own strident brand of patriarchal *power-over*, and foment their own ruthless attacks and retaliatory actions, such as the Taliban, Al Quaeda, and the myriad of off-shoot and independent terrorist organizations threatening the world today.

In the *power-over*, egoist organizational context, the role of the person in charge is to confirm that everyone is following the prescribed course of action, while guarding against mistakes and applauding loyalty and certitude. Thus, the old model with its focus on control made absolute clarity and certainty king, thereby denying the role that mystery and uncertainty play in fueling creativity and making space for differences which in turn make cultures rich and civility essential. When leaders are obsessed with unquestioning obedience and coherence they spend extra time worrying about maintaining complete control and clarity, and tracking any deviations from the imposed vision. Rather than inviting collective problem solving, and innovative risk-taking, someone is blamed when something goes awry, which in turn establishes division among followers and fertilizes the ubiquitous organizational "rumor mill." Within the *power-over* model, while the leader's rhetoric may eloquently express the value of teams and cooperation, the fundamental reliance on positional power in fact yields little to the collective in any way that truly values partnership and collaboration.

In the *Partnership Model*, the alternative presented in these pages, leadership emerges at the confluence of creativity and constraint, where people come together to participate fully and practically in shared expressions of service to expanded definitions of both "progress" and "success." In this context, leadership is drawn away from a preoccupation with maintaining power over others, and away from narrow assumptions that unimaginatively assert that leaders are only those with some monopoly over, if not some preoccupation with, perfect rationality, consistency, and coherence. In later chapters, we examine power within the partnership context, the qualifications for the Partnership Leader, the need for community leadership, and a program for leadership training that emphasizes dialogue, stewardship, and service as visions and goals are enacted and accomplished.

Patriarchy Frames our Institutions: Government, Religion, Economics, Education, Science and Technology, and Health Care

In order to change baseline understandings and use of leadership and power, it is important to understand the strength of the operating system that provides the context and the structure for virtually all American organizations. That system, based on a mythic storyline parallel to that of the hero, is the patriarchy, which is an institutionalized social *system* based at its core on egoism, narcissism, and assumptions of scarcity, which result in a perceived need and justification for competition, domination, and control. In this context, patriarchy refers to a system of control, not just those who hold power (the patriarchs), be they men or women.

The patriarchal, or *power-over* system could not have lasted so long and had such an overwhelming impact on our definitions of "good work" if it had not resonated with both men *and* women; clearly it has in some way met the needs of both for a very long time. Therefore, we are all culpable for sustaining the prevailing system and we find it difficult at this point to imagine an alternative capable of overcoming it. Yet, the needs of our times are changing, and replace it we must. Given that this biased and limited worldview was collectively shaped in a variety of expressions emanating from human societies around the world, then we are equally capable of crafting a viable alternative that is built on a foundation of full, fair, and evenly balanced participation and partnership.

In the process of working to move beyond the *power-over* system, there is a temptation to get sidetracked from the work of cultural change by entering into academic arguments about differing versions of history and particular qualities of prehistoric societies. In that respect, regarding theories of how the established system was generated, Allan Johnson allows, "Maybe it all happened this way and maybe it didn't. But our inability to prove where patriarchy came from won't stop us from reaching our own conclusions about it" and working to change things. The work is needed at both individual and organizational levels. Johnson insists, "We can't just focus on individuals; we also have to find ways to focus on the *system*" (*Gender Knot* 124). Furthermore, he argues, "Patriarchy isn't problematic just because it emphasizes *male* dominance, but because it promotes dominance and control as ends in themselves" (249). Competition, domination and control can be both seductive and addictive—both for anyone who attains power *over* their fellow workers or society members and for the subordinated members who perceive that they might someday occupy the power roles—and have their turn on top. Thus, Johnson concludes, it is important to understand that "all forms of oppression draw support from common roots, and whatever we do that draws attention to those roots undermines *all* forms of oppression" (249). This concept represents an important thread in this work, in that by developing some sense of how humans might have gotten into this fixation on competition, fear, and control, which often devolves into oppression—we can also develop some sense of a way out.

Since the various and overlapping human rights movements in the 1960s, there has been growing recognition of the widespread negative effects of the patriarchal system. Social science researcher Cynthia Cockburn, in *The Way of Women: Men's Resistance to Sex Equality in Organizations,* notes, "If the United Nations Decade of Women, 1975-1985, did nothing else it demonstrated the reality of patriarchy" (6). She further explains, "The opening years saw the assembling of detailed evidence of women's subordination around the world; the end of the decade confirmed just how hard it was to change anything. Patriarchy was real and it was durable" (6). Not only is patriarchy real, it exhibits all the characteristics of an entrenched *system*: it is structured, extensive, highly stable, and capable of self-reproduction. Clearly, changing the core operating system of a culture—including an organizational culture—is no small undertaking.

Ironically, patriarchy's enduring capacity for self-preservation does not equate with it being beneficial at more than a temporary or superficial level for anyone but those who are in control. In that respect, at this point in human history, the vast majority of those who hold power have systematically—albeit sometimes unconsciously and without malicious intent—disenfranchised millions of people. In spite of myriad efforts to make some headway against this powerful system, disenfranchised millions of men and women, minorities and indigenous populations, have little hope of changing their fundamental circumstances, and many of the helping organizations themselves struggle with and are hindered by internal egoism, authoritarian systems that support power struggles, and competition among themselves.

Even in the face of mounting evidence of long-term, widespread, behind-the-scenes corruption, there is cause for hope. Addressing the systemic difficulties in current American society, Johnson argues, "The patriarchal paradigm weakens in the face of mounting evidence that it doesn't work" (*Gender Knot* 239). For those who rely on evidence from mainstream business publications, the current system appears to be working; the top-down, hierarchical, and authoritarian paradigm neatly supports those on the top of the heap—the "fathers," even though some are women—while solidly sustaining their command, control, and narrowly-defined (and often unsustainable) profits, to be shared with stockholders but rarely trickled down to frontline workers.

This system ruled by "patriarchs" (whether male or female) has not been truly working for many women and other disenfranchised groups—including minorities and undereducated men—for a long time. Members of those groups are often at the receiving end of command and control dictums, and their participation has been constrained by a variety of mechanisms. Furthermore, one after another, key institutions in the infrastructure ruled by modern patriarchs—e.g., "captains of industry," powerful political "bosses," and righteous church leaders—have in their egoistic quest for self-aggrandizement and narcissistic gratification betrayed their constituents' trust. The very revelations of deception—coupled with a viable partnership alternative—provide grounds for hope that a system that thrives on secrecy is unraveling.

While there have been many revelations in the past few years of betrayals by those in charge of organizations throughout our society, only a few examples are included here for illustration. While industrial capitalism maintains class domination, revelations of widespread financial mismanagement by corporate power-abusers have sent shock waves throughout the marketplace. Feeble government attempts to corral lucrative campaign financiers meet with rhetoric and tokenism that attempts to mask stiff opposition to change from complex multinational organizations and the increasingly monopolistic mass media. Changed regulations passed by the Federal Communications Commission in June 2003 ensured further domination by the corporate elite by removing government restrictions on media monopolies. While Congress initially rolled back those changes, they were then quietly slipped into the "Omnibus Spending Bill" for fiscal year 2003-2004. The net result of that amendment coupled with political operatives posing as reporters means that ferreting out the "truth" in the midst of increasingly partisan journalism is becoming ever more elusive.

The interlaced economic system that has become a global marketplace has been developing a vast, self-beneficial network since the advent of the Industrial Revolution. This system is integrally interwoven with the system of *power-over* competition and control. As Johnson contends, "What changed the world was not mere capitalist industrialization, but patriarchal capitalist industrialization." That distinction applies in a wide array of cultural frameworks. Johnson explains that even "the socialist alternatives that developed in response to capitalism, such as in the Soviet Union and China in many ways represented little more than a new form of competition between patriarchal systems" (*Gender Knot* 44). Within the American context, the system has moved forward to become the *corporatist* patriarchy. In that respect, large corporations provide the predominant organizational working model, and it is often difficult to see that there could be and indeed there is another way of operating.

In the scientific arena, organizational biases surfaced with revelations that the bulk of medical research has drawn conclusions based on subject populations who have been comprised consistently and exclusively of male participants. As Riane Eisler, futurist and codirector of The Center for Partnership Studies observes, this fact means that "most policymakers work with only half a data base" (*Chalice and Blade* 175). Those disclosures have finally led to new studies on the differing effects of drugs, surgery, and even stress on the female body and psyche. For example, UCLA researchers Shelley Taylor and Laura Klein conducted an extensive review of the medical literature on the effects of stress in a study funded by the National Institute of Mental Health. They found that men tend to respond with "fight or flight," and women prefer to "tend and befriend"—results that contradict long-held, gender-neutral assumptions regarding stress responses, and have implications for adjusting a wide range of other behavioral assumptions.

Further research on the effects of allopathic ("Western" drug and surgery-focused) medicine on the female body have revealed shocking failures in science-based technology that panders synthetic hormones to menopausal women that have been shown to be harmful after all. Oddly, some of these same researchers are now touting as "new discoveries" alternative, holistic plant-based treatments known to indigenous and wise-women healers for centuries. Additional admissions that several popular drugs approved by the Federal Drug Administration, including Celebrex and Vioxx, can have serious, previously known but undisclosed side effects, have cast a shadow over the safety of medications licensed by a theoretically unbiased federal agency that has become closely linked through practice and legislation with pharmaceutical companies.

In case the crisis of confidence in the scientific, economic, and corporate arenas was not enough, the religious arena, where many people place their faith and trust as a source of integrity and justice, has had its share of scandals. For example, a widening circle of disgrace involving pedophile Catholic priests initially shielded from prosecution by church hierarchy was later shown to be an elaborate cover-up (Lavoie). This powerful Catholic bastion of religious tradition is intimately related to the Judeo-Christian patriarchal foundation myth that serves to protect and defend its own, and is also a strong proponent of the ongoing, systematic exclusion of women from positions of leadership. As literature professor Carol Lee Flinders observes in *At the Root of This Longing*, "Organized religion has been no great friend to women" (325). Indeed the foundational story of the fall from grace, held as a disastrous consequence of Eve's "original sin," has been used as the justification for the blame, mistreatment, exclusion and subjugation of women for thousands of years. In keeping with that belief system, as recently as 2001, the conservative Southern Baptist convention declared a return to its earlier restrictions — based on narrow interpretations of Biblical teachings — forbidding the entry of women into their ministry. The Church of Jesus Christ of the Latter Day Saints, more commonly called Mormons, has always prohibited women from the priesthood and relegated them to auxiliary functions. Thus, as women and other minorities have sought to expand their participation in mainstream organizations, dogmatic religious institutions have often conspired in restricting their access.

At the core of these organizational control systems, the very process of innovation and change itself has been called into question. As philosophy professor Carol Ochs asserts, "Much of Western philosophy from the pre-Socratics through Plato and Aristotle has been concerned with humanity's inability to deal with a world of change or transformations and a desire for a world outside the domain of change" (49). Indeed, once it achieved hegemony, the orthodox Christian church has done everything within its considerable power to maintain the status quo by feeding dependency on certitude. Ochs reminds us, "Patriarchal religion and philosophy have focused on the changeless" (57), or on maintaining the constructed status quo in order to preserve the inflexibility, secrecy, power and control that protects their vested interests (Iogna-Prat; Eire). This focus on preservation of a shielded status quo also reflects a profound dislike for ambiguity, and an accompanying willingness to forego needed changes in order to avoid having to deal with uncertainty around outcomes.

In the political arena, threats of further terrorism within the bastion of America itself are being met with "more of the same," escalating displays of *power-over*, and attempted control at home and abroad, even when precious resources and civil rights are sacrificed in the process. Externally, American military might all too often catches innocent noncombatants in the crossfire and leaves vulnerable local populations at risk of long-term health effects from huge swaths of denuded land and aquifers permanently contaminated with carcinogenic elements (most recently in Afghanistan and Iraq). Internally, governmental control over public records and citizens' movement is escalating and eroding principles of privacy, freedom of expression, and dissent that are hallmarks of our democratic ideal.

Following that trajectory, in many arenas the system of *power-over* domination is requiring ever-increasing infusions of regulation and punishment in order to remain in control. Yet legions of fearful people, who either lack an alternative vision or are protecting their vested interests, staunchly support the patriarchal status quo. This fear-based defensiveness was evidenced in the 2002 American elections, when the party of the President made historic gains in both houses of Congress, in spite of social unrest and economic distress (e.g., falling stock markets, increased numbers of unemployed or under-employed workers, corporate corruption scandals, and looming budget deficits). A discouraged electorate largely refused to participate in the decision-making process, resulting in poor voter turnouts in many areas, which meant the elections were decided by a small percentage of eligible voters. Seeking to build on the previous triumph of that strategy in the 2004 election, the Republican party once again successfully focused public and media attention on war and fear-based stories, while effectively minimizing the attention given to domestic issues such as health care, employment issues, and the growing need for alternative energy sources that would reduce dependence on (and depletion of) foreign petroleum sources. Another strike at securing the future with an educated citizenry was dealt by inadequately funding its much-touted program that promised to "leave no child behind" and canceling the Pell Grants that had assisted many low and middle-income students in completing a university degree.

In response to these conditions, psychology and philosophy professor Richard Tarnas and psychologist Murray Stein suggest that the time has come for the predominant "hero myth"(based on the image of the lone wolf) to shift into the "myth of relationship." This story-line shift replaces the hallowed American individualistic image with one based on recognition of interdependence between people from all nations, ethnicities, and faith traditions, and of the profound need for collaboration. Rather than focusing on the rugged individualism of the hero going out to take over the world by wielding brute force and defeating the "evil doers," the myth of relationship focuses on the hero's return to the community with the treasure—whether that "boon" be increased self-knowledge, a more global perspective, or some tangible, measurable fortune—gained on the road of trials. In the myth of relationship, the focus shifts to challenges involved in operating in *service* to, rather than in *control* of, and in seeking cooperation with others, rather than requiring compliance.

For those who have been schooled in the ways of the *power-over* tradition, these may be foreign concepts, because they are either ignored or suspiciously denigrated as potentially "collectivistic," "socialistic," or even "communistic" by those who promote the dominant system. Nevertheless, they are important concepts, and the willingness to explore them is escalating as the breakdown in the effectiveness of the current system is becoming increasingly apparent.

By re-visiting our core cultural myths and proceeding with what the eminent Swiss psychologist Carl Jung called "moving the myth forward," we can discover new interpretations of old stories and new visions of the way things could work. Then individuals can gain a sense of hope that things can be different. This process provides a foundation for working together to co-create organizational and societal programs that address the deep structural changes necessary to make a massive course correction.

Of course there are many questions that arise with the contemplation of making these changes and the subsequent transitions. They include:

- What will be the pattern of the new myth (or myths)?
- What threads are needed?
- How can they be spun?
- How will the balance of tension be accomplished for the weaving of a new cultural fabric, and for weaving a world that works for all?
- What might be the catalyst to cause these changes to take place?
- Who will provide the leadership for this paradigm shift?

These questions are addressed in subsequent chapters of this book.

Because the challenges inherent in this cultural transformation are immense, the transition from patriarchal *power-over* to partnering *power-with* will be challenging, and will require tenacity, cooperation, and communication skills unfamiliar to many. Perhaps the most difficult aspect of this transition, particularly for a culture with a generally low tolerance for ambiguity and an obsessive need for absolute order, clarity, and certitude, will be the inability of anyone to predict the final pattern of the new myth or the new relationships made possible when conscious partnership replaces unconscious individualism. Historian Gerda Lerner, in *The Creation of Patriarchy,* assures us that "we are no more under an obligation to describe what we will find than were the explorers sailing to the distant edge of the world, only to find that the world was round" (14). Nevertheless, the challenge to change the way things are compels this work.

"You have set sail on another ocean without star or compass, going where the argument leads, shattering the certainty of centuries." (Kalven ii)

Organizational Versions of the Patriarchal System

As the early patriarchal system advanced from a family-centered dynamic and radiated to the king-subject relationship, it became firmly established in the socio-political and religious arenas. It was a simple progression for evolving institutions to adopt the rules of command and control as well. Enter the Industrial Revolution.

The eighteenth-century Industrial Revolution represented a profound sea change in the ways work was accomplished, goods were produced, and women were involved in that production. "Before industrialization," Allan Johnson explains, "there wasn't much that women couldn't and didn't do, and husbands and wives depended on each other for their survival" (*Gender Knot* 42). He further emphasizes that the same class domination of European feudalism (which was based on military force, land control, and obligations between nobles and peasants) gave way to industrial capitalism, where "class domination is based primarily on control over complex organizations such as corporations, government, and mass media" (41). Thus, in spite of the profound shift in the mechanics of production, the threads of domination and control continued to define the social fabric.

There was another important aspect to the evolution of control, which contributed significantly to the status of men within the system. Johnson suggests that after the Industrial Revolution, "the position of the father lost so much of its traditional authority" with the shrinking family sphere of influence that "the gender system was no longer patriarchal but androcratic, based on male (*andro-*) rather than father (*patri-*) dominance" (42). Cockburn observes that "the effect on the patriarchal status of the working-class family man was painful" with the advent of wives and children working in the factories in order to save the family from destitution. She explains that the "home and factory became twin spheres in which a working-class man's status relative to women had continually to be reasserted" (78). In the process of asserting that status and control, the structure morphed from a relatively simple system within the family and community to a complex "religion of power" (Johnson 43). Thus, while in some respects the "religion of power" was enforced from external socio-political sources, in other respects it also manifested in compensatory behavior within family and community relationships, thereby expanding its pervasive influence.

Centuries later, the advent of mass media exacerbated the situation, in that television and movie images portrayed an illusion of an attractive nuclear family ideal, rather than the reality being experienced in thousands of homes. That illusion in turn became an icon; it was a goal to be cherished and held up on pedestals of privilege. Unfortunately, the belief that more than those at the top echelons of society could actually attain that world also engendered frustration, bitterness, and cynicism, even as it veiled serious and wide-spread dysfunctional behavior and relationships.

In the organizational context, the "religion of power" is reflected in the strict hierarchical structures, top-down decision-making policies, separation of workers based on status and technical demarcations, and limited roles assigned based on relative positioning within the standardized pyramidal organizational chart. As Johnson explains, "Roles are sets of ideas about what is expected of people based on the positions they occupy in social relationships" (66). Within the classic organization, the most valued roles are at the top of the pyramid, and correlating interpersonal styles require that the players involved show "emotional detachment and the appearance of *in*vulnerability in order to enhance and protect their position in a system based on control and domination" (65). Thus many individuals believe that they must maintain a certain detachment in order to effectively supervise those at lower ranks of the pyramid. Physicist and former Oberlin College President Robert Fuller, labels this arrangement of organizational relationships as "rankism." In *Somebodies and Nobodies: Overcoming the Abuse of Rank,* he notes, "Since hierarchies are pyramids of power, rankism is a malady to which hierarchies of all types are susceptible" (4). Rankism in turn sustains a matrix of privilege that includes as facets race, gender, sexual orientation, class, religion, and ethnicity. Each facet is often portrayed as a separate issue, and yet when viewed through the prism of rankism, *power-over*, and control, their interrelationships within the "religion of power" become readily apparent.

This stew of roles, power, styles, privilege, and an implicit sense of male entitlement all too often result in gender privilege in the allocation of both positions and wages. Thus, even in 2004, American women still make only 73 cents to every male dollar, and the percentage of women in leadership roles remains low (Utne). Private researcher Molly Shepard, principal of The Leader's Edge, reports that based on their research, although there is some perception that "the old 'glass ceiling' has been cracked, as of 2002, the 'Boardroom Barrier,' which affects women reaching for the highest levels in corporations, is shown to be intact" (www.womenof.com). Additional studies conducted by the Annenberg Public Policy Center at the University of Pennsylvania reveal that at the end of 2003, "women still comprise just 15% of executive leaders and just 12% of board members in top companies. These numbers are virtually unchanged from the previous year" (www.annenbergpublicpolicycenter.org).

For some, that inherent gender privilege extended and abused becomes sexual harassment. When that situation is challenged with legal action, the frequent response of many organizations is to hire more women (usually as a result of court-ordered mandates), make a scapegoat out of the one "bad apple," and/or require standardized "diversity" or "sexual harassment" training for all employees. These actions frequently force rankism into a latent underground, where resentments smolder and passive-aggressive behavior sabotages organizational initiatives. In order to move beyond us-and-them dichotomies that harbor envy, cynicism, and outrage, this particular dynamic merits careful attention and deeper responses than superficial and mandated training programs.

This state of affairs presents an admittedly difficult conundrum: the needed changes are about much more than just "add women and stir" (Flinders, *Rebalancing* 172). As a consultant to a wide variety of organizations, I have often heard the accusation that many women who are hired for top management jobs are accused of "only getting that job because they're a woman." Allan Johnson refutes this complaint by noting, "When men complain about the advantage some women gain from affirmative action, they ignore centuries of pro-male affirmative action" (*Gender Knot* 159). On the other hand, I have also observed that some women have indeed been hired to fill a court-mandated quota, even though they were sadly lacking in the necessary experience, networks, or expertise to be effective at the job. Unfortunately, whether intentional or not, they have often either not been given the kind of training and mentoring that could have supported their growth into competent managers, or the men they were hired to supervise are required to train them. Rather than address the underlying relationship issues, both of these situations sabotage their success, undermine the effectiveness of organizational initiatives, and compound the difficulty of the overall circumstances.

Many women who were able to enter the ranks of upper management were expected to conform to traditional models of management control, whether or not they had the aptitude, adequate experience, or access to training or mentoring. All too often, they found there was very little room for innovative management practices. Indeed, in many traditional organizations, "the path of least resistance for managers is to mentor and promote people who most resemble themselves, which in most companies turns out to be white men," or are people who at least mirror images of the white male style (Johnson, *Gender Knot* 243). Therefore it follows that many women (and minority men, who may have very different approaches to supervision and problem solving) who have attained top management levels have found it necessary to adopt the mannerisms and language of command and control in order to break through the glass ceiling, fit in, and be taken seriously. As Johnson notes, "It is easier to allow a few women to occupy positions of authority and dominance than to question whether social life should be organized around principles of hierarchy and dominance at all," or to "question whether people's needs should depend on an economic system based on dominance, control, and competition" (*Gender Knot* 13). The organizational culture change required in order to shift these management attitudes and practices can only be completely effective throughout the organization when it is embraced by top executives who adopt, model, and encourage it.

Thus, the greatest challenge lies not in superficially changing the gender balance of the workforce (in order to get the numbers officially "right"), but in changing the core organizational culture, which is comprised of a (usually implicit) mixture of policies, procedures, roles, and norms: the operative behavioral agreements between organizational members.

As Johnson describes organizational culture, "The minute you walk in the door, you can feel yourself stepping into a set of relationships and shared understandings about who's whom and what's supposed to happen and why, and all of this limits you in many ways" (77). This restrictive (yet often implicit) characteristic of organizational culture is particularly important, since as organizational consultant and management professor Peter Block observes, the prevailing cultural system of competition and control "is fueled by its need for predictability" (24). That predictability is often married to survivability, and the intrinsic fear of failure that often accompanies proposed changes. Both predictability and perceived survivability rely on "legislated accountability," which in turn "creates compliance and caution" (26). Subsequently, that reliance on compliance and caution creates the rules-based bureaucratic mindset, which in turn "breeds self-centeredness and self-interest" and depends on certitude and consistency (26). Furthermore, bureaucracy sustains the directives of the patriarch, who is rewarded for legislated compliance with tenure and control. It is extremely difficult to introduce flexibility, creative innovations, or true teamwork within this kind of cyclical and fear-based organizational culture.

Yet even for all the complaining about bureaucracies and the self-interested bureaucrats who run them, Block notes that rather than seek a better system that might break the cautious predictability cycle, we all too often "believe we need a better patriarch" (26). For many employees, focusing on factors that are external to oneself, such as a CEO who is believed to be poorly performing or an economic downturn, is much easier than examining the company's core culture and myths, especially for cautious, compliant individuals who do not have a vision of an alternative. By abdicating or not understanding their responsibility to participate, many people actually collude in keeping the *power-over* system of competition and control in place. Thus, the patriarchal system remains entrenched and grows likes weeds in a garden, through culpable neglect and tacit approval.

Jungian analyst James Hollis also contends that a "common way to avoid the burden of consciousness is to relinquish it to the group or Great Leader." This occurs in both small and large-scale contexts; as Hollis observes, "We have seen entire nations relinquish their individual consciousness and moral values, following charismatic leaders on holy rampages" where the pursuit of power and "the lure of groupthink is all too evident" (114). In the organizational context, even though many workers have a sense that things could be better, they seek to pin both blame and hope on someone else, perhaps in the past, or at another level of society, or on the organization itself. On the other hand, Johnson asserts that it is essential to realize that everyone "shares responsibility for any system we participate in, whether or not we had a hand in creating it" (221). Admittedly, the concept of shared responsibility is far removed from most workers' experience.

Most people can recall experiences where the "person in charge" demanded full allegiance to his or her view of reality and what would work or not work. Interestingly, that dynamic does not always occur within an overtly *power-over* system. For example, a project manager who talks the talk of teamwork, only to respond curtly to individuals' suggestions with variations of "No! That will never work!" is generating neither teamwork nor partnership. What is demonstrated in that instance is disrespect or public humiliation, under the cover of positional power. When group members become discouraged (or fearful) with the prospect of offering ideas or suggestions, and feel that they have been demoted—not officially, but in a de facto manner—to merely "staff," their participation tends to be less enthusiastic. This often leads the manager to wonder why he or she has lost input and support, and to engage in external blame by accusing the group members who did not fully acquiesce or willingly support the imposed vision of "not being team players."

The "team front" in the *power-over* organizational culture is a façade too often supported by banal managerial rhetoric and hoisted upon the workforce at periodic teambuilding opportunities. No wonder so many employees are disillusioned at work when the very "ropes course" intended to develop team-ness can leave them caught in a Gordian knot of frustration over insincere attempts at sustained participation. When this occurs, those mountaintop experiences of community and team spirit quickly fade, and the result is often disappointed cynicism and lowered morale. Too often teambuilding initiatives raise hopes, which are dashed upon return to the office environment. As a result of this kind of disappointing experience, some clients have occasionally asked me to refrain from using the word "team" during conflict management interventions.

These organizational formats and expectations are so pervasive that they infect the very image of what "team" means, and many people cannot conceive there might be another arrangement that could work. Indeed, Allan Johnson observes, "We're so used to the patriarchal obsession with control that it's hard to imagine that a society might exist without a dominant group" (*Gender Knot* 46). Likewise, many people have a difficult time comprehending that a group does not have to have *a* leader; it can be a group of *all* leaders, who all take responsibility for the outcome, all work synergistically, all share in the decision-making and all share in the work. Yet there are examples where this kind of "shared leadership" works, including members of the Religious Society of Friends ("Quakers"), who have been demonstrating the efficacy of this model for centuries. These dynamics are further addressed in chapter 5.

Many organizations have tried to implement shared leadership programs in a quest to elicit more participation and higher profits. Unfortunately, these efforts have for the most part only addressed the edges of the underlying inequality inherent in the organizations. For example, *Total Quality Management* (TQM) and *Continuous Improvement* programs are often bolstered with interpersonal and communication skills training and teambuilding efforts. In Johnson's opinion, these efforts combine to create a "myth of a kinder, gentler capitalism in which managers still overwork and lay off employees in order to bolster the bottom line and protect shareholders' interests; but now they do it with greater interpersonal sensitivity" (*Gender Knot* 82). From my experience and observation, rather than relinquish control, they also sometimes employ covert co-optation in an effort to enlist the workers' participation in their own demise. Nevertheless, for all their short-comings, early efforts at *Quality Circles* and teambuilding have produced increased awareness of both the possibilities with increased employee engagement and of the pitfalls inherent in experimental programs led by individuals who were trained in techniques, but have not always had adequate understanding of the changes they were trying to implement.

Thus, a fundamental challenge in transforming organizations includes the will and commitment to nourish personal leadership capacity in everyone, and to change consciously and collectively organizational systems and cultures in order to support truly collaborative approaches.

Of Shadow and Light

Admittedly, my original intent in pursuing this research was to demonstrate the sins of the patriarchy and to showcase the pleasures of partnership. As I began my research, I committed the sin of dualistic exclusivity by casting the sides as polar opposites: the big bad patriarchs versus the virtuous new dawn of supportive, collaborative alliances. Over the course of my work, I discovered that each system shares a common feature: they are both comprised of both *light* and *dark* sides. In other words, at different times and in different places, each side has had its ascendancy and value. Thus, while the patriarchal system, or "rule of the fathers," has certainly been the source of much of the world's prejudice and pain, it has also provided the structure for great advancements in the fields of science, technology, and political movements. Therefore, before proceeding with turning fully to the partnership system, it is important to unpack both sides of the patriarchal system.

When I was a child, my mother would caution me that sometimes our greatest strengths, *when taken to excess*, eventually become our blind spots and worst shortcomings. In that vein, it is feasible to consider that the patriarchal system was not necessarily started with outright domination as its goal. Indeed, it may have come forth as an impulse for creating order, clarity, discipline, and rational problem solving in response to chaotic social changes and the specter of scarcity in the face of growing populations. Nevertheless, under Eurocentric and Americentric forms of governance it has been widely taken to excess and devolved into a systematic quest for domination, characterized by rigid rules and pervasive laws. Those rules and laws, many of which terrorized the non-ruling class during the Middle Ages and were subsequently used to justify European colonialism, slavery, and genocide on all continents, still live on as baggage from those earlier times. Although controls provide comfort for rulers or "fathers" (who, it must be remembered, were occasionally women) in the patriarchal system, they were by design stifling and too often downright harmful for everyone else.

There are several particularly cogent examples of possible patriarchal "good intentions" that have long since devolved into self-interested domination. What may well have started as an attempt to provide compassionate care for the "flock" by a benevolent provider has morphed into an all-out effort to gain and maintain control within a win-lose paradigm. In this game, as emphasized by attorney Lani Guinier in *The Tyranny of the Majority: Fundamental Fairness in a Representative Democracy*, the winner takes all. Although lip service and token funding may be given to social programs, the poor are for the most part left to fend for themselves. Furthermore, the original impetus to provide collective protection against invading hordes or environmental catastrophes, which required courage and loyalty in an "us against them" situation, has all too often degenerated into separation and *othering*. Within that frame of reference, "us against them" has infiltrated the very core values of a fear-based worldview. In the resulting polarized universe, there are the *good folk* and the *evildoers*. Individuals and groups innately claim the moral high ground for themselves; they are the *good folk*, and others are by definition held apart as the "them." "They" are the evil ones, the enemy, the wrong-headed group that shapes by seemingly natural negation the first group's privileged corner on the market of what is good, right, and true. Within this frame those who are labeled as different are then experienced as enemies, who must be converted, conquered, or destroyed.

When stirred by the heroic urge for exploration and adventure—admittedly laudable human actions—the impulse has repeatedly been hijacked whereby victory brings with it gross patriarchal exploitation, ranging widely, for example, from nationalistic colonialism and imperialism that seek to control local resources to economic and social abuse of uninformed, powerless welfare mothers. Those same single mothers are often painted as greedy charlatans and are conveniently blamed for their inability to "pull themselves up by their bootstraps," with the message that they do not *deserve* the largesse bestowed upon them by the benevolent *fathers* of society. Those *fathers*, by projecting their own greed onto disenfranchised groups, then proceed to stridently lobby in favor of a smaller government that is less capable of intervening in their operations and requires less tax revenue. They set about to achieve those goals by curtailing or canceling meager benefit programs while simultaneously increasing the government's capacity to wage even greater victories and protect more vigorously the property—and power—of the ruling class.

After centuries of being labeled inferior and kept from the halls of power, women may carry cellular memories within their collective unconscious that manifest as an *inner patriarch* who whispers incessantly "You're not good enough," further limiting their own exploration and progress, and thereby curtailing their potential as contributors in organizations (Stone; Woodman, *The Ravaged Bridegroom*). Meanwhile, those grand patriarchs in charge depict themselves as superior beings, heroic leaders, and "compassionate conservatives," even though their policies regarding children, the elderly, the homeless, and the natural world reveal painfully and practically how they are neither compassionate nor conservative, neither superior nor heroic.

Are there still some situations that call for a parental figure to care for those who are not able to care for themselves or willing to take responsibility for improving the situation? Most certainly. Yet, just as some petty dictators have declared martial law to stem the tide of rising violence in the streets and then retained that condition indefinitely because it afforded them exclusive control, the rulers of the patriarchal, *power-over* system have also over-extended their privileges. The patriarchs stayed too long and discovered absolute power that has absolutely corrupted even the best of their intentions. While patriarchs maneuver to maintain an aura of invisible privilege clothed in manifest destiny, those privileges are now being enjoyed at the expense of both the governed and of the earth's vulnerable ecosystems that are expected to support humanity indefinitely.

Seeking Cultural Transformation

*To imagine how things might be, we first have to get past the
idea that things will always be the way they are.
We have to be willing to travel without knowing
where we're going.*
(Allan Johnson, *Gender Knot* 236-237)

Much has been written in recent years about the need
for radical transformation of our culture. Feminist scholars,
in particular, have examined the creation and impacts of the
patriarchal myths and systems in a variety of contexts. There
have also been studies based in archetypal and depth
psychology, mythology, and organizational theory
addressing the fundamental changes both needed and already
occurring in some organizational structures, policies, and
leadership. These studies have been largely motivated by
efforts to increase access to basic civil rights, along with
ever-increasing organizational complexities, global
economic demands for increased flexibility, and escalating
incidences of international and interethnic warfare, all of
which call for increased cross-cultural sensitivity and
peacemaking efforts. Many studies have tracked the need for
managing transitions as groups attempt to navigate the
wilderness between the status quo and a proposed new, not
entirely clear model. I have woven together perspectives and
resources from each of these areas in this book, with an
emphasis on applications to the organizational context, and
to partnering relationships.

One hopeful view of potential cultural change is
presented in *The Cultural Creatives: How 50 Million People
are Changing the World*, wherein values researcher Paul Ray
and psychologist Sherry Ruth Anderson provide hope for
profound cultural change as they present the results of
thirteen years of research on American values. They explain

that there are now three main cultural value-oriented groups in the United States. *Traditionals* seek a return to "the good old days," where values were presumed clear and strict rules and laws were tightly enforced (such as the romantic conservatives' illusion of the past). *Traditionals* believe that by strengthening the prevailing patriarchal, *power-over* model, the conditions of the "golden" past will be restored. *Moderns*, on the other hand, base their hopes on progress and the growth machine, fueled by unending growth and development, worship of the powerful magic of technology, and careful, scientifically engineered strategic planning.

Ray and Anderson identify the *Cultural Creatives* as a newly emerging, third cultural group that values ecological sustainability over economic growth and development. This group prefers not to be bound by rigid hierarchies, as they seek collaborative and creative solutions and build intentional circles and collaborative communities. The authors contend that the *Cultural Creatives* are poised to have a significant impact on American politics and economics, but that they currently are mostly unaware they are members of such a large group, and are therefore as yet less effective in promoting changes to the current system. (For a checklist of *Cultural Creatives'* characteristics and priorities, see *www.culturalcreatives.org*.) Mobilizing this group will be an important facet in moving into the proposed partnership paradigm, as discussed in later chapters.

The very notion of transforming an organization—let alone an entire culture—can be overwhelming, especially when faced with *true believers*. Those who favor absolutist mentalities focus on scripted belief systems that deliver precious certitude, which often cause them to miss subtle nuances in systemic oppression and opportunities for change. Yet Johnson maintains, "We don't have to go after people to change their minds" (239). More and more people who truly understand the systemic problems and acknowledge their personal responsibility in either unconsciously perpetuating or resisting changing the system will awaken and change their own minds. Some will remain wedded to a worldview forged in an ethnocentric cultural myth that portrays domination and control as justified by self-identified—and self-righteous—moral superiority. Although these individuals cannot be forced to change their minds, they can at least be encouraged to expand their perspectives regarding differences and possibilities.

Those who have a vision of another way of operating do need to step out in front of the pack, refuse to collude in the continuation of a domination-based system, promote an alternate vision of what is possible, and support newcomers to the movement with ideas, encouragement, and inclusion. Groups can begin by creating dialogue circles and support communities that function in a coordinated way to both protest injustices and develop new answers. Transformation is possible in spite of corporate monopolies with vested interests in maintaining *power-over* hierarchies, or fundamentalists waging a backlash against women and minority groups seeking to share power, or widespread fear that paralyzes progress toward these fundamental changes. In part this transformation is achieved by providing training and consistent mentoring that builds personal leadership capacity and communication skills in both organizations and schools. It is also achieved by carefully reworking core organizational power structures, so that many people, rather than a few at the top, are genuinely empowered and stand ready to take responsibility for helping navigate our organizations and communities through the necessary transitions.

Americans especially need to provide leadership in creating organizations that support unusual thinking by promoting and engaging in open dialogue that not only tolerates but actively invites differences of perspectives and opinions, rather than attacking those who see things from different angles or make different interpretations of events and conditions, and dismissing them as "evildoers." Veteran journalist Bill Moyers has been at the forefront of this kind of in-depth research, analysis, and reporting, by carefully revealing the important questions that should be asked, the underlying structures that withhold critical information, and the players who stand to profit at the public expense. Moyers stands as an elder in American culture. Hopefully he will continue to inspire us with his wisdom and challenge us with his searing questions, even though he has retired from full-time journalism.

This call for a cultural transformation at the root level of our organizations represents a fundamental shift in how we relate as human beings. This is an opportunity to weave a new pattern of *inter-being* that calls forth our deepest desires for meaningful work, for positive, productive relationships based on mutual trust and respect, and for creating a hopeful future. By understanding the stories or myths that underlie our individual and collective efforts, and the roles that they require, we can begin to make conscious choices, expand the frames, and co-create new stories. Then we can develop a model for co-creation that involves building mutual trust and respect at the core of our relationships and organizations, as explored in the next chapters.

Some might dismiss this worldview as a hopelessly optimistic perspective. I assert that it is indeed idealistic (which differs significantly from simplistic optimism), in that it calls upon our highest values and ideals. It is also very practical, in that *it works*. The partnership paradigm offers a container within which we can have the conversations about what the world *can* be, including how we *can* get along and have respectful dialogue, even when we disagree, and that at the end of the day we *can* work through our problems together. It takes the committed effort of each individual, who realizes that each effort does in fact make a difference.

❧ Chapter 2 ❧

Awakening the Potential of Partnership

There is an enormous need both to reveal the deceptive and destructive nature of the prevailing system and to provide an alternative vision for operating in radically different, responsible ways. In response to this need, various movements have emerged in the past few centuries, which while seemingly unrelated, all carried a common goal: To challenge the narrow traditions of domination.

Riane Eisler points out in *The Power of Partnership*, "The 'rights of man' movement of the seventeenth and eighteenth centuries . . . challenged a tradition of domination: the 'divinely ordained' rule of kings over their 'subjects'" (94). Since that compelling tear in the *power-over* façade of domination, a number of other movements have arisen, each with a particular focus on challenging aspects of command and control. Thus, the feminist movement challenged the control of men over women, the abolitionist movement challenged the control of White people over Black people, and the pacifist movement challenged the use of "force as a means of one nation to control another" (95). The twentieth century brought movements to humanize the treatment of the mentally ill, to challenge corporal punishment of children in the schools, and to institute fair wages and safe working conditions. All told, a variety of movements arose, each seeking to protect and defend rights of the disenfranchised against the practices of those who assumed dominion over all things.

These movements, some better organized and larger than others, have each focused on generalized civil rights along with the rights of specific groups (e.g., indigenous peoples, gays and lesbians, those who are "differently abled," senior citizens, and the on-going concerns of women). Those concerns range from voting rights to the right for a woman to choose what happens with her own body and to avoid violence in intimate relationships. Finally, Eisler notes, the environmental movement "challenges the once-hallowed conquest of nature," or dominion of humankind over the earth (94). Collectively, in spite of often-fierce resistance, these movements have succeeded in raising a nascent awareness of the collective effects of domination practices, and of the need to devise another way of operating.

In spite of the efforts of these movements, in these early years of the new millennium, most organizations remain stuck, couched securely within structures and traditions that reify the *power-over* system. They are structured around hierarchies of competition and control, which by design curtail employees' opportunities to participate fully in the operation of the organization. Yet if either employees or leaders decide not to play by the traditionally competitive rules anymore, they will find few guidelines for how to organize differently and may feel marooned in a sea of conventional practices. Nevertheless, there is a growing belief that corporations are just as capable of having beneficial effects on both society and the natural world as they are of causing social havoc and environmental damage. Indeed, the sustainability of business—socially, economically, and ecologically—is emerging as one of this century's central debates. To this end, the shifts required to change that paradigm at the organizational level leads us to ask:

- How would Partnership, as an alternate operating system, inform and assist organizational changes appropriate to these times?
- What organizations offer examples where non-patriarchal operating systems have been successfully implemented? What are the metrics

that define their "success" or sustainability? And how do they operate differently from traditional institutions?

- How does partnership sustain a balance between creativity and constraint?

The Partnership Model

Partnership represents a radically different model from the long-established system of competition, *power-over* domination, and control. Diane Kennedy Pike, diversity trainer and creator of the "Life as a Waking Dream" workshop, asserts, "Partnership challenges the old rules. Instead of absolute power being held by the head of the family [or organization], power is shared among peers." This notion is confusing to many people, who cannot conceive how power could be fully *shared* because most of us have never experienced it and are at pain to imagine it. Pike explains, "Authority is no longer automatically attributed to the few in positions of power. Instead, authority is acknowledged as belonging to all, with respect to their own lives and futures" (2). We thus "author" our own life.

The principles of partnership include respectful, civil communication, even when there is disagreement, shared influence and *power-with* rather than *power-over* control and competition, and a focus on connecting, relating, and collaborating, rather than separating, hierarchical "rankism." In turn, relationships freed of the dynamics of *power-over* are able to develop within a consciously crafted climate of balance and mutual respect. Even with widely differing levels of skill and experience among the members of any organizational group, partnership can work. Partnership is *not* an attempt to generate sameness, thereby sinking to the lowest common denominator, or denying the expert contributions of any organizational members. Partnership *is* a paradigm where each voice is honored and heard with respect, even when there is disagreement. Heterogeneity, not homogeneity, fuels the complement of perspectives and talents that make partnerships valid and necessary, and make collective progress truly possible.

Thus, rather than promoting the expectation to put up, go along, and act in the *power-over* version of the "team player" blindly supporting the will of the ruler, partnership actually provides a container for asking questions and for fully engaged participation that promotes both individual and collective growth, which provides a whole new framework for understanding what it means to be a member of a "team." As Eisler explains, relationships based on the principles of partnership "enable us to grow mentally, emotionally, and spiritually." Furthermore, partnership is not limited to organizations, but "is true for individuals, families, and whole societies" (*Power of Partnership* xv). While a true partnership does *not* guarantee everyone getting what they want or threaten becoming mired in a stalemated consensus process, it *does* involve patient listening so that group members are sincerely *heard,* disagreements are handled without personal attacks or rude dismissal of individual inputs, and there is a guarantee of genuine involvement in the process of reaching an outcome.

Since many organizational leaders who are interested in changing the climate and culture of their workgroups turn to external resources for assistance, it is important to distinguish between popular teambuilding events and fundamental transformation into the *Partnership Model.* Those leading teambuilding efforts may have knowledge of the latest games and techniques, but lack the wisdom and experience to fully comprehend what they are trying to do. When managers or in-house trainers are given only rudimentary training to use various style instruments or to present canned teambuilding initiatives, they do not have the depth of experience and understanding to be able to handle adequately some difficult situations that crop up. That situation can be scary and frustrating for the presenters as well as the attendees. Consequently, the very people who organize and present these events are sometimes themselves more disillusioned than anyone at the lack of positive, lasting outcomes. Unfortunately, as well-intentioned—and fun and entertaining—as many team-building initiatives may be, they may be also conceived as quick fixes that are all too often misdirected, misunderstood, and ultimately not supported with adequate follow-up. At its foundation, teambuilding— and partnership—is about building trusting *relationships*, which must be developed over a period of time, and cannot be rushed in a one-time teambuilding event.

Relationships at every level can be transformed by adopting the *Partnership Model.* When the relationship at one level shifts, there are ripple effects throughout all of the other levels, whether the relationship is with one's co-workers or one's significant other, within the organization or the community. At an individual level, those who exercise self-respect and discipline in their diet, their sleeping patterns, and their exploration of emotional and spiritual aspects of themselves are less likely to accept quietly or condone abusive treatment at work or the reduction of their civil liberties by governing bodies. Couples who are committed to building a partnering relationship that rejects the co-dependent, abusive, soap-opera models widely portrayed by Hollywood, the media, and in popular music, while building mutual respect and trust, learn patterns of relating that can carry over to the workplace and the community. Within a committed relationship that operates as a partnership, John Robinson, a psychologist active in the men's movement observes, "The respective journeys of each partner, however great or difficult, feed the relationship, and the relationship, in turn, feeds the journeys" (37).

Consequently, rather than separating the home life from the work life and from the well-being of the community, individuals who commit to their own personal path of growth and collaboration nourish each successive level of relationships.

Personal, organizational, and social aspects of change are intimately connected. Consequently, parents who carefully attend to and are involved *as partners* in all aspects of their children's education—the social, emotional, and spiritual, as well as the intellectual arenas—find that by responsibly engaging in, *without having to dominate,* the learning process, the family and the entire community benefit. Adults who offer their time, skills, and energies as volunteers in local organizations—whether or not their family benefits directly—add to the web of support for those who need a helping hand. As anthropologist Mary Catherine Bateson observes in *Composing a Life: Life as a Work in Progress—The Improvisations of Five Extraordinary Women,* "Building and sustaining the settings in which individuals can grow and unfold, not 'kept in their place' but empowered to become all they can be, is the task of parents and teachers, and the basis of management and political leadership" (56). Thus, communities that provide support for families and conscious learning opportunities for new parents, new teenagers seeking their "place," and new elders seeking to contribute the wisdom learned (and earned) from their experiences, also provide a context within which partnership can grow at the most basic levels.

In the larger context, families who seek out locally grown, whole foods both re-establish a connection with the earth and the ecosystems of their communities and live in partnership with their neighbors who grow the food. In contrast, foods shipped enormous distances undermine local agriculture, and require petrochemical fertilizers and other products and processes to increase shelf life, and massive consumption of petroleum products to ship in off-season produce rather than changing dietary components to match the seasons. (Admittedly, the United States Food and Drug Administration has yet to establish consensus among growers, grocers, and consumers as to what constitutes *whole* or *organically grown* foods.) Operating in partnership is also expressed through *glocalization*, or participation in truly *fair markets* (as opposed to *free markets* that primarily benefit large corporate entities) and the cooperative governance of both local communities and the world community. Biologist Elisabet Sahtouris argues that *free markets* are free for those who stand to gain the most, and that their gains are most often at the expense of small entrepreneurs. For example, many economists in assessing the impact of the North American Free Trade Area (NAFTA) on the tenth anniversary of its passage now acknowledge that small family farms in both the United States and Mexico have suffered tremendously under a trade agreement that promised otherwise. In contrast, larger corporations merely shifted production and supply chains to other countries (e.g., China) as labor costs rose as a result of NAFTA, thereby protecting their profit margins, contributing to the ascendancy of Chinese presence in world agriculture, and sealing the doom of any pretense of a true international partnership that "lifts people out of poverty," as has been promised.

At the most basic, everyday level, those who consciously conserve their use of water and energy resources and carefully recycle wherever possible, whether individually or at the corporate level, act in partnership with the earth and with all of humanity as they contribute to the protection and sustainability of planetary resources. These kinds of actions protect the potential that those resources will be available for the benefit of all people on earth—not just a wealthy few who have squandered the fresh water, productive soil, and petroleum products and then cornered the market on control of the precious remains.

Those who reach out to new immigrants with welcome and succor, or who reach out into the world community either by volunteering themselves or supporting organizations that provide on-the-ground disaster and developmental aid are partners in the world community. Fortunately, as expressed in many local efforts to clean up streams and preserve open spaces, to increase recycling participation and extend mass transit options, and to donate millions of dollars to disaster victims, both at home and abroad do demonstrate, many people are already finding ways to incorporate partnerships into their lives, even though we live within a this-or-that, dualistic and hierarchical society. This is the behavior that deserves applause, reinforcement, and extension into the workplace.

Such efforts also highlight reconnections in areas of life that have been systematically disconnected under the established system of separation, ranking, competition, *power-over*, exclusivity, and domination. That system is intimately entwined with an absolutist, hierarchical mindset, based on the premise that certain things are the exclusive responsibility or dominion of the home, the school, the religious setting, the government, and so on. Within that mindset, everything has its place, and the arbitrary assignment of that place by those "in charge" is not to be questioned. In this way obsessive-compulsive disorder becomes institutionalized; a culture of obsessive-ness punctuates not simply individual behavior, but social order that is ironically and cruelly maddening to those who seek to change it.

Unfortunately, if these handed-down classifications remain unquestioned, and their *power-over* authors go unchallenged, our communities suffer a hardening of the categories. We begin to believe that there is no other way for things to be organized; that this is "the way" and any attempt to change the way is itself an invitation to disorder, chaos, or worse (we are told) catastrophic social decay where received truth is crushed by the evil of disorder. There are inflexible, simultaneous designations that other things, such as education in music, art, and communication skills—all of which promote critical, systemic thinking and relationship building—are unworthy of support in "hard times."

Within that hierarchy, individuals have traditionally been expected to separate their work and home personas. Early in my work career, we learned quickly that it just was "not professional" to allow home concerns to interrupt one's workday. The contextual shift from the traditional system of competition and control to the *Partnership Model*, on the other hand, supports and encourages realigning the mind with body, spirit, and soul, and reconnecting one's personal and work lives by consciously integrating partnership principles at all levels. This integration is impossible so long as an individual continues to accept as the only reality the harsh polar division between work time and the rest of life, and thus surrenders the best hours of the day—and the bulk of their days—to the corporation. Fortunately, shifts in this aspect are becoming more and more acceptable and common: day care centers and breastfeeding rooms are integrated into workplaces, the Family Leave Act supports family concerns beyond simple maternity leave, and business magazines post and applaud annual evaluations of "family friendly workplaces."

Adopting a partnership philosophy and practice involves shifting from an exclusive system emphasizing rank-based constraint and control to one that invites widely creative, varied, and even contradictory opinions and ideas, while consciously preventing exclusive control by any one self-absorbed and egotistical group with its narrow unimaginative ideology. Partnership in any group setting also requires shifting from a regime of command and control that depends on secrecy, coercion, and compliance into a system that obligates openness and responsibility for all members. Additionally, partnership educates for and rewards involvement, and it consistently seeks both the participation and the willing support of all members in the organization or the society. When those fundamental changes are instituted, then there can be a conscious and careful reweaving of the previously severed threads of community.

The expression of true partnership represents a radical shift from the dominant paradigm of elaborate social role stratification and individualistic competition. Thus, even as there are glimmers of partnering behavior in various arenas, adopting full partnership across the board is difficult and even frightening for many Americans to imagine. This is partly due to the cultural backdrop in which we are bathed in media images of strong-arm action figures, schooled in pervasive competition, and raised with a Disney version of father-dominated families. When presented with the possibility of incorporating partnership models into their organizational frameworks, many Americans dismiss it as "pie in the sky" or only allow, "it's a great idea," but lament that "it will never work."

Acknowledging such pervasive pessimism, Eisler and Loye caution, "It remains exceedingly difficult for organizations, even if they started along partnership lines, to sustain such patterns when surrounded by a larger society and culture that is determinedly and oppressively 'dominator' in style" (167). Nevertheless, as Ray and Anderson present in *The Cultural Creatives*, and Margaret Wheatley describes in *Finding Our Way,* there are millions who are actively seeking an alternative to both the traditional and modern variations of the patriarchal system. They are coming together in a variety of formats, ranging from small local "circles" to work-related teams that consciously seek to rise above the tokenism of mere "team" labels, to community coalitions that bring together previously disconnected or competitive groups. There is a growing number of diverse international gatherings that work to build bridges of understanding, such as the "Interfaith Dialogue Gathering," held in Washington, D.C. in November 2004 and the "Gather the Women" Congresses held in Dallas and San Francisco.

Characteristics of Partnership Organizations

There is a growing body of evidence that partnerships can be and are successful, even in the face of strong dominator resistance. Organizations that are functioning within the partnership paradigm generally tend to share a common set of characteristics, as outlined by Riane Eisler and Alfonso Montuori in *The Partnership Organization: A Systems Approach*. They note that partnership organizations have flatter, less rigidly hierarchical structures, and that where hierarchies do exist they are "hierarchies of actualization" that encourage innovation, flexibility, and individual initiative. The role of the manager is dramatically changed "from 'the cop' to a facilitator" who provides "transformational and empowering leadership" that seeks to help workers develop their full potential (2). At the core, the concept of power within a partnership organization is changed from coercive, *power-over* manipulations that operate at the expense of others to generative, *power-with* relationships that seek to identify and implement the most effective ways of working together to solve problems. This concept is further explored in chapter 3.

Partnership organizations view the human beings who work within them very differently than do traditional, hierarchical organizations. Strictly hierarchical organizations consider workers to be resources—albeit *human* resources—that can be exploited for the benefit of the organizational entity, and when they get burned out, they can be easily replaced with younger, less expensive, more malleable *cogs* in the wheel. Partnership organizations, on the other hand, consider workers as people to be nurtured, mentored, and valued, not as mere personnel or even as "human resources" to be used, disposed of, and replaced.

Rather than perceiving human diversity as a threat to established order, Eisler and Montuori propose that diversity be reframed as an opportunity, which provides "greater creativity and innovation, new perspectives . . . and presents possibilities for unusual and generative cross-pollinations," (4). They report that redefined, permeable gender roles are particularly important, in that "individuals who are not trapped in rigid stereotypical gender roles tend to be more flexible and psychologically healthy. They also tend to find it easier to work with others in teams rather than merely assuming positions in rank orderings," which too often reflect traditional gender stereotypes (4). I have found that increased respect and valuing of diverse perspectives greatly improves the organizational climate.

These changes in the way the organization regards its workforce are beneficial in that workers who experience more supportive, flexible ways of perceiving and interacting with others at work are less likely to resort to high levels of absenteeism and turnover as coping strategies, and more likely to experience high levels of morale and productivity. Since recruitment and training costs of new employees are rising, retention is becoming ever more important to the organizational bottom line. Turnover and retention data indicate that many people leave to find other work largely because they do not feel *valued*, and one of the top reasons people are fired is insubordination. Both of those indicators are directly affected by shifting to partnership principles.

All of these changes in turn address the tremendous drain that hampers the effectiveness of many traditional organizations: office politics. Eisler and Montuori call office politics the "vast, unspoken shadow that hangs over all organizations" (3). They believe that by changing the dynamics of power, shifting from top-down management to collaborative leadership, and instituting true team approaches, office politics—fueled by finger-pointing, blame, and murky manipulation—can be at least seriously limited, if not eliminated altogether. They also caution, "Creating a partnership organization requires a deep re-organization of our beliefs about what it means to work together. Challenging assumptions is a key ingredient of the creative process," which includes exploring "the very way we think" and the "mental traps" that lead to "polarized thinking" and the "us against them" of office politics (5). Addressing office politics requires shedding light on its myriad manifestations and concurrently providing everyone with skills and understandings to counteract its effects, if employees expect to dramatically change the valences of power and leadership within the organization. Exploring and implementing changes in power and leadership, which are key elements in the move to becoming a partnership organization, are further addressed in chapters 3 and 4.

Fortunately, excellent examples of applied partnership already exist, as is apparent in a growing number of model organizations across a spectrum of American society. There are resources for those interested in partnership parenting; schools that offer collaborative, experiential learning models; and organizations that have consciously dismantled top-down authoritarianism while providing on-going training in communication, partnering, and alternate problem-solving and conflict transformation models. As Eisler notes, "The movement toward partnership is at the heart of innumerable causes," which "transcend conventional categories such as communism versus capitalism and religious versus secular," even though, without a name or commonly recognized identity, this movement is not widely reported in the media (*The Power of Partnership* xxi). In the interest of examining both the successes and challenges of organizational partnerships, a variety of these applications are reviewed in chapter 5.

Before examining those organizations, it is important to consider potential limits to their development. Does partnership also have a *shadow* side? Yes, in that without careful elucidation, strongly supported meeting agreements, and consciously amplified communication, facilitation, and conflict management skills, the illusion of partnership provides those who would passive-aggressively pretend to support needed changes—but still seek to manipulate and retain control—with yet another mechanism for holding the group hostage. Indeed, I have encountered some group leaders and organizational managers who fluently speak the language of partnership while actively derailing efforts to achieve it. In those cases, if the individuals charged with providing oversight to organizational programs and initiatives are unable or unwilling to operate in true partnership, their efforts to change the culture often result in a sham. Therefore, it is crucial to provide guidance and mentoring in partnership principles at all levels of the organization, or within a unit with a defined span of control.

For example, operating in consensus represents a dramatic change from vertical chains of command, where workers are often denied the opportunity to fully participate in identifying company values, a shared vision, or strategic goals. Yet consensus itself can be abused, when universally applied, and can be a confusing and difficult methodology. Eisler cautions, "We must be careful not to confuse a partnership structure with a completely flat organization or one where everything is run by consensus" (69). Indeed, within a strict consensual framework those persuasive, controlling managers who hold the threat of retaliation can easily manipulate those who do not fully understand the principles and processes involved in operating in full partnership, or who do not trust the new paradigm.

In any situation, I have found that using consensus can be very perplexing without training in dialogue and facilitation. Without attending to fundamental assumptions, stories, understandings, and commonly accepted behavior standards, organizational members who are new to full participation can all too easily fall into the trap of *groupthink* or get caught in the mire of planning and decision-making that still reflects fundamental turf protection. When that occurs, even as those same managers loudly proclaim their allegiance to the so-called "teambuilding efforts," they demand adherence to their version of partnership or team principles and subsequently co-opt employee trust. Understandably frustrated employees then dismiss this latest effort to change how things work as simply another fad without lasting substance, or as "management by best seller."

The fear for those considering a move away from dominator hierarchies and into partnership is that there will be chaos, anarchy, and the failure of a structure-less organization. At its heart, people fear a lack of predictability and control. Top managers will ask, "How will we get anything done? How do you expect us to run a profitable business?" Rank and file employees likewise fear the lack of order, asking, "What am I supposed to do? How will I know that I'm doing a good job?" In that context, powerlessness and lack of control—and the potential for failure—become synonymous.

That fear exposes the overwhelming suspicion of anything that challenges the prevailing order, no matter how flawed we all believe it to be. It also calls the question on how little we understand about creating and sustaining true partnerships. Knowledge of partnerships coupled with the skills in open communication—particularly in listening and perception checking—are the antecedents to our shared progress. As Eisler and Loye make clear, "Non-hierarchical (not based on a dominator hierarchy) does not mean structureless. Nor does it mean that everyone has to be paid the same or do the same thing, nor that all tasks—including managing—are rotated among everyone" (166). Given those common misunderstandings, it is easy to see how fears of rampant turmoil, not to mention more obsessive beliefs in the threat of unfathomed and maligned socialism, cause insecurity among those faced with major changes in operating systems. For this reason, the movement to true partnership organizations requires not only knowledge and skill, but also imagination and courage.

There has, in fact, been a steady stream of efforts to introduce some of the partnership modalities into organizations in the last several decades. Unfortunately, without widespread understanding of the underlying principles and how they interact with cultural norms—or the will to relinquish opportunities for self-aggrandizement and control—those efforts have often been co-opted and subverted. For example, *Quality Circles* (originally called *Quality Control Circles*) represented a program that engaged workers in processes of collective solution-seeking that first found success in Japan, where they were introduced by Edward Deming, an American statistician interested in applying quantitative models of predictability to quality control and employee involvement.

From the early 1970s and into the mid 1980s, U.S. manufacturers enjoyed the high financial returns arising from cost-saving ideas generated from *Quality Circles*, but they did not in the long run support greater expansion of employee involvement. In some cases, *Quality Circles* (QC's) were introduced to thwart unionization or to use group pressure to force greater productivity. Instead of changing organizational culture, the *Quality Circle* movement in the U.S. reinforced managerial control and corrupted the movement to such a degree that today *Quality Circles* often signifies insincere, faddish efforts to involve people at work and unethical human resource manipulation of work groups. Today, QC's would seem anathema to partnership; minimally the QC movement taught us that skill training of group members and leaders and opportunities for conversation alone are insufficient for the realization of the structural and cultural change required in the organization. Further, experience has shown that disguising manipulation and coercion will eventually be unmasked.

More recently, efforts to reduce discrimination, prejudice, and *othering* by providing superficial *diversity training*, while providing some consciousness-raising, have largely resulted in increased rules, litigation, and a variety of quick-fix anti-harassment training programs in a culture bent on externally controlling behavior without supporting basic, long-term attitude shifts. Likewise, even though those who sincerely want to effect changes may initiate expensive teambuilding initiatives that all too often involve superficial game playing, while guardedly avoiding the deeper issues thus keeping the group stuck in dysfunctional, competitive relationships. In that instance, groups might enjoy the "mountaintop experience" of the event, but little changes. At this point, as both corporations and federal agencies create parallel budget slush funds for settlement agreements with disgruntled employees, they even discard any appearance (or hope) of even attempting to "fix" the underlying problems.

The unfortunate result of these programs in many organizations is that little changes at the level of attitudes, beliefs, and norms. As a result, even though the underlying concepts are valuable, *quality*, *diversity*, and *teambuilding* become widely dismissed as ineffective processes for fundamental change, and are largely considered superfluous. The terms have all too often come to represent little more than techniques, used superficially to give the illusion of teams and partnership, while hiding the deeper strategy that continues to deny full participation. To be sure, there are many individuals who have benefited from their training and teambuilding experiences, and who have managed, even in the midst of power-over organizations, to integrate team and partnership principles into their daily lives and their working *modus operandi*. They have been able to create "pockets of partnership" in their workplaces, and they demonstrate that in order to build true partnership, technique alone is not enough, and integrity is requisite.

The result of these experiences has been a realization —in some quarters, at least—that partnership does not work by merely changing organizational structures, titles, and policies. Furthermore, as Eisler explains, "a more partnership-oriented culture doesn't mean a laissez-faire, everyone-do-what-they-want style in a totally horizontal workplace. On the contrary, it involves clear expectations, standards, and guidelines" (*Power of Partnership* 73). Rather than external imposition, partnership is an inside job. Eisler continues, "What it can mean is that all individuals in an organization are there by choice, and take part in decisions as to what role they play, how they work together, and how the work and the organization are structured" (166). In order to incorporate those levels of involvement, there must be a complementary, coordinated effort to examine and change the attitudes, beliefs, actions, and norms within organizations in order to support fully the proposed new structures and policies. This deep work cannot be accomplished by relying on games and techniques; it requires going into the *underground* of the organizational culture, clearing out old conflicts and misunderstandings, and re-working the usually implicit operational agreements—the norms—by making them consensually derived and explicit.

The shift in cultural consciousness from competition and control to partnership and collaboration provides an opening through which some will choose to move toward true partnership. Whereas many organizations have been operating in a self-absorbed, privileged, and strictly profit-based manner, the critical need is to recognize the wide-ranging community costs and the larger environmental impacts that these narcissistic, *power-over* organizations have wrought upon all of our lives through their policies and actions. Acknowledgement of those costs and impacts carries with it the responsibility for making deep changes in fundamental cultural and organizational structures.

Strategies for Organizational Culture Change

Where to begin? Five initial strategies help people move toward partnership organizations and make possible the necessary deep organizational culture changes:

• **Create structures that support webs of inclusion, rather than hierarchies of exclusion**, so that all voices can be heard within the programs and practices of the organization. Employees at all levels of the organization can attend to the structures—be they involvement in meetings or opportunities to have input to agenda-setting—and to implement those structures by consciously incorporating widely varied voices. This is a key difference reflected in the guiding metaphors that inform different ways of constructing organizations. Sociological researchers Mary Field Belenky, et al, in *Women's Ways of Knowing,* describe the differences between hierarchical pyramids or mountains, where one or a powerful few dominate the many at the bottom, and images of webs of interdependence, where "no one position dominates over the rest" (178). Therein reside helpful clues to achieving the potential of the partnership alternative. More in-depth information is given on how to structure and achieve these "webs" in chapters 5 and 6.

• **Give high priority to maintaining open and mutually respectful communication**. Partnership organizations provide training for everyone to develop skills in communication, understanding of intercultural dynamics, conflict management and transformation, facilitation and mediation, and collaborative decision-making. Everyone—beginning with the leaders of the organization—consciously works at modeling active listening and open communication that supports building mutually respectful and trusting relationships, even when they disagree. It is particularly important to note that active listening becomes the purview of everyone, and not just the responsibility of those at lower rungs of the organizational ladder who have traditionally been expected to listen to their "higher ups," without necessarily being listened to in return. If there is any doubt about whether communication skill-building initiatives are working or are merely producing "lip service" results, check the tone in the organizational climate and the quality of the relationships between employees; if both have improved, partnership efforts are having the desired effect. (If, on the other hand, sarcasm and "office politics" are thriving, more work is needed in this area.) More information about specific training elements is included in the case study of the NEFA Agency, presented in chapter 5.

• **Re-structure reward systems to reflect congruent support for team efforts**, rather than solely rewarding individual "stars" or limiting the reward recipients to managers who take personal credit for the work of those "below them." Given the cultural propensity for promoting individualism and competition that results in winner-take-all results, this is perhaps one of the most difficult changes for many Americans to comprehend, and a challenge for managers as they contemplate reward structures. As Joan, a manager for a large food and beverage processing company observes, "I have dealt with patriarch bosses—the military style, using telling instead of dialogue, fear, and little rewards—but found that they don't really tell someone they're doing a good job because they assume they 'should' be doing it anyway." Rather than believe the stereotype that only older, well-established bosses hold to this style, she remembers, "I've also seen some young people who are like that. They are dictators who tell people what to do, tend to be hovering micromanagers who don't trust people, and if anything goes wrong, they jump to blame, which promotes secrecy and deception." In the interest of creating partnerships, she notes, "If I get those types within my organization, I have to weed them out." Joan has found that sincere recognition goes a long ways in promoting a balance between both individual and collective achievements.

I have observed that changing the reward system so that whenever possible, all team members receive recognition for exemplary service and team achievements— rather than richly rewarding the manager for the work of the group under them—goes a long way toward fostering a sense of a partnership organization. In the experience of the NEFA Agency cited in chapter 5, successful rewards were not always necessarily monetary or individualized. Sophia, the NEFA Executive, explains the key, "You need to know what makes people happy. If you first care about people, and can cut them in on figuring out what can be done, you can find out what they are good at, and reward them by supporting their strengths. For example, you can provide opportunities and time off for them to attend classes, and then put them on the agenda to talk about their experiences and share their learnings, or have them provide trainings for their colleagues, and proceed to praise them publicly."

In this situation, competition is reframed from interpersonal or even inter-group competition to striving for continual improvement, as stated by the 4-H motto, "To make the best better." More specific details of team compensation are beyond the scope of this book, and can be found in resources such as *Compensation for Teams: How to Design and Implement Team-Based Reward Programs,* by Steven Gross. As Sophia states, the key lies in getting to know what makes people happy—and understanding that it's not the same for everyone.

• **Accept and encourage expression of other "ways of knowing."** This is certainly not to say that organizations would abandon *logos* (rationality or intelligence); such a move would represent a ridiculous swing of the pendulum to the opposite pole. Partnership organizations recognize multiple ways of "knowing," and seek to incorporate and balance *logos*, *eros* (emotions), and *pathos* (intuition) into their development, decision-making, and planning; thereby operating within a continuum, rather than between polarized dualities. Within this paradigm there is a "connected knowing, that arises out of the experience of relationships... its [primary] goal is understanding, not proof" (Belenky 183).

There is also a deep honoring of in-house wisdom that integrates knowledge, experience, and process-based flexibility that is reflected by listening to input from non-traditional sources, at more than a token level. This shift can also be achieved by reframing interactions. For example, rather than lecturing to an audience, there is what Belenky, et al., refer to as "a conversation with colleagues, working on questions that matter to all of us," and realizing that we are "working on a process" that is a living, dynamic progression (xxi). This also includes accessing and promoting the *emotional intelligence* that psychologist, journalist, and past Harvard faculty member Daniel Goleman notes accounts for almost 90 percent of what sets leadership stars and change catalysts apart from mediocre managers, and makes the difference between *emotional intelligence* and *emotional incontinence* (186).

• **Respect and honor diverse perspectives and opinions**, whether based on cultural, ethnic, gender, socio-economic, political, religious, age, ability, or functional differences, thereby honoring different "realities." Rather than operating within a system that portrays itself as "the reality," recognize there are many realities, each of which merit consideration. For example, seek out attitudes and behaviors that reflect both feminine and masculine perspectives, and then encourage and reward their expression. This course of action replaces browbeating employees with superficial anti-harassment training, which tends to drive xenophobic and homophobic attitudes and *othering* behavior underground, where it is more difficult to alter. There are also enormous potential rewards for the organization, in that energy that had been previously tied up in defending individual rights to hold and express unique perspectives is unleashed to focus on realizing organizational mission, performance goals, and profitability.

Being in partnership certainly does not involve taking the easier path. It does require discipline, commitment, and the willingness to admit mistakes and re-group, rather than charging blindly forward in order to "win" or even to "save face." This represents a dramatic shift in the consciousness and behavior of many Americans. Indeed, Houston believes that in the process of moving beyond the myth of the hero-patriarch, we are called to "co-create an entirely new order of being" (*The Hero and the Goddess* 378). That "order of being" is built on inclusive integrity, accountability, and stewardship that are woven into transformed organizations. Americans in the twenty-first century have the opportunity to build a society based on those principles from the ground up: beginning with our relationships, whether in the home, at work, in the community, or abroad.

*Out beyond the ideas
of right and wrong doing
there is a field.
I'll meet you there.*

& Rumi

☙ Chapter 3 ❧

The Paradox of Power
in Partnership Organizations

Reframing Power and Conflict

In order for an organization to move fully from the traditional system of authoritarian control to realizing partnership principles, it is critical to understand the key differences within each system relative to how power is distributed and how leadership is manifested. This chapter examines the differences between the system of *power-over*, which is based on domination and control, and *power-with*, which is based on collaboration and relationship-based teamwork.

By way of introduction, any relationship that operates from a basis of *power-with* is distinguished by (1) sharing and cooperation (rather than competition and turf protection); (2) treating conflicts as learning opportunities and seeking win-win outcomes (rather than perceiving conflicts as destructive, winner-take-all struggles); and (3) focusing on ways to re-humanize individuals (rather than dehumanizing them). How do individuals and organizations manage to shift from one system to the other? Since the current *power-over* model is so omnipresent that it is virtually invisible for many people, the place to begin is by clearly understanding the genesis and characteristics of the traditional power orientation in order to spot the places where it crops up, and then to learn how to consciously replace it with an entirely different approach.

When many people think of power, they envision armaments and military might, or various incarnations of political, economic, or social control. Yet power is also a very personal issue. Sociologist Marilyn French, in her classic 1985 treatise *Beyond Power* observes, "Even when power is defined as domination, the term is murky and dependent on personal prejudice" (505). There are layers of both personal and cultural filters regarding authority, influence, and control that color perceptions of powerfully influencing or managing various situations, even when behaviors are attributed to an ideal of protecting the common good. In Americentric societies, power is generally considered a good thing to "have," and an indicator of one's personal worth. In a society where power is equated with control and is perceived as a benefit, demonstrated by protecting against the hordes at the gates, French notes, "Those with the greatest power are considered the 'greatest' men," who are often accorded wide berths in wielding their power (506). Particularly in times when profound fears are stirred—whether of terrorism or the perceived failure of values-based institutions—and threats or disaster seem imminent, power holders are not only allowed, but are expected by many to exercise any option they deem necessary to guard the citizenry.

It is during unsettled times that powerful patriarchs are most often able to extend their control and latitude, particularly if they choose to fan the fires of public fear. Some argue that it is precisely because such unscrupulous bosses have taken advantage of public hysteria that domination should be eliminated. Nevertheless, French concedes, "Coercion —domination—is not eradicable. It is impossible to envision a world in which some form or degree of domination is lacking" (506). Even within groups who sincerely wish to operate in partnership, there is the potential to implicitly exercise *power-over* and hold the group hostage by manipulating the group norms, agreements, and decision-making processes. Those who call for what archetypal psychologist James Hillman names the "tyranny" of "the absolutism of equality" (99), must admit that in an organizational context that tyranny often emerges in the guise of one who is calling for equality at all levels, and "talking the talk but not walking the walk;" they promote teambuilding and partnerships while simultaneously denying full participation by those who would be their partners.

On the other hand, at times there is indeed a need for someone to "take charge" and make pronouncements regarding organizational programs and processes. For example, in the beginning of the NEFA organizational transition into partnership described in chapter 5, there were times when the agency Executive had to definitively state that even though their path through transition was confusing and difficult, going back to the old ways was not an option. The key difference between the dictators and hard-line executives who rule with an iron fist and the partnership leader who makes the call when decisive action is required, is that the former retains firm, often micro-managing control under *all* circumstances, and the latter recognizes that power can be fluid, rather than locked into a particular position, and seeks to relinquish control as much as possible, in favor of shared decision-making and problem solving. This approach nourishes the capacities of everyone in the organization to grow a sense of shared power, which in turn unleashes energy and creativity, and contributes to the synergy of the whole.

Power at the personal level is often demonstrated when someone who possesses a particular knowledge, skill, or personal charisma acts to apply their abilities. The source of personal power can be as widely divergent as a brilliant Albert Einstein, a skillful heart or brain surgeon, or the profound compassion of Mother Theresa. Personal power linked to building relationships has been eloquently demonstrated by renowned peacemakers, including Mahatma Gandhi, Martin Luther King, Jr., and Rama Vernon, founder of Women of Vision and Action and The Center for

International Dialogue. Following the lead of these exemplary individuals, and increasing our understanding of relationship power can provide some clues for the quest to change power dynamics in order to support and enhance partnership.

Tracing the allocation and the flow of power is an essential element in the redefinition of the parameters of authority desirable for an organization or a society. This redefinition is critically important because, as organizational theorist Peter Block insists, "If the issues of real power, control, and choice are not addressed and renegotiated, then our efforts to change organizations become an exercise in cosmetics" (27). The threads of partnership (i.e., *power-with*, *shared* vision and leadership, and building community) are integrally linked in moving beyond unsustainable "window dressing" exercises and directly speaking to the grasping domination of the *power-over* system.

The concept of shifting the way we operate in our relationships with each other at every level of our lives requires that we must fundamentally learn to change the way we understand and hold the notion of power. For power does not exist in isolation; it is intimately tied to every layer of relationships and has immense impact on every aspect of the organizational milieu. French writes that from her viewpoint, *"To have power* really means to have entry to a network of relationships in which one can influence, persuade, threaten, or cajole others to do what one wants or needs them to do" (509). In that context, power is born out of our longing to affect our own lives and the world at large, and thus holds enormous potential for our nourishment or destruction.

The way power is conceptualized and used is key to understanding the differences between traditional authoritarian and partnership organizations. Within every organization relationships are continually brokered, whether in open, participative, and democratic ways, or in the *underground* of self-interest, deceit, and collusion where power is wielded as a weapon for gaining control and compliance. Whichever their heritage, when those relationships are examined for their interdependencies, a web becomes apparent: one woven strand by strand, just as a spider creates her web, with the purpose of netting whatever is perceived as "food" for the individual or the organization it benefits. When considering those organizational webs, several questions arise. They include: Who wove this web? What was the weaver's intent? What has been the impact of the web's design? What alternative designs might be more beneficial to the organization?

The *power-over* model is one that has been growing and reinforced over the course of many centuries. Social change activist Starhawk explains, "Power-over, or domination, is . . . the power of a small group to control the resources or to limit the choices of others" (*Webs of Power* 6). This is the power formula with which we are all very familiar, and which French believes is predicated on either "eradication or domestication" (507). Eradication involves murdering one's opponents (either metaphorically or literally), and has been used strategically through the millennia, as examples from the Old Testament, the records of the Holocaust, and more recent terrorist communiqués attest. The dysfunctional logic with eradication is that it calls for an unending cycle of destructive conflict and revenge with the goal of eradicating all enemies, failing to acknowledge that such an effort actually makes more enemies along the way and ultimately means having no one left to dominate.

On the other hand, domestication requires education and persuasion to the prevailing ideology, and must be supported by various forms of ever-escalating control, including imprisonment, punishment, intimidation, and surveillance. The problem with domestication is that the rulers can never be fully certain they have attained full control over those they are seeking to dominate. As French concludes, "The dominators of the world never have a day off" (509). The cycle of desperation continues.

In case there are any doubts regarding how power-over works in the organizational setting, organizational consultants Robert Greene and Joost Elffers have delineated a set of forty-eight *laws of power*. They contend, "The game of constant duplicity resembles the power dynamic in the scheming world of the old aristocratic court . . . which was supposed to represent the height of civilization and refinement" (79). These *laws of power* from the Middle Ages are critical to the success of *power-over* dynamics, and have been well preserved by a long line of patriarchs and their functionaries.

Understanding these *laws of power* can serve both those who lust for power and those who sense a need to defend themselves against their use. Although many of the laws are well known ("conceal your intentions," "learn to keep people dependent upon you," "discover each person's thumbscrew," etc.), Greene and Elffers caution that some passive-aggressive power strategies give the appearance of cooperation, while masking the true motives of the perpetrator. These strategies are often particularly difficult to disarm. For example, Greene and Elffers note, "Treating everyone equally means ignoring their differences, elevating the less skillful and suppressing those who excel" (79), which results in an organization that breeds a culture of mediocrity, yet ensures that the power mongers remain in control because they have created an illusion of fully-equalized democracy that the more talented fear to challenge and the less skillful prefer.

Another "effective means of deceit" is the use of naïveté, because it disarms one's opponent by calling on their sensitivity to help those who appear weaker or less fortunate. This strategy may also appear as claimed inability to participate, and is another common variation of passive-aggressive manipulation. By withdrawing into seclusion or refusing to participate in the conversation, in order to avoid another's displeasure, individuals (powerfully) contribute to the disruption and disintegration of dialogue. This roundabout tactic in itself can become a game of destructive one-upmanship.

An additional arena where many people abdicate their power by refusing to participate lies in the right to vote. School children in the U.S. are taught at an early age that they live in a democracy in which each person has the right to participate in the process of governance by voting, which represents an important opportunity to effect the direction of the sole remaining "superpower" nation. My parents reinforced this lesson by teaching us that voting is a sacred right, duty, and powerful opportunity that we should cherish and never dismiss lightly, even when we do not care for the choices available. When individuals disengage by not voting (with excuses that "my vote doesn't count anyway," or "I don't have time for jury duty"), or by abdicating responsibility and choice to someone they perceive as a "savior" or "hero-patriarch" who will tell them what to do, they give away their power.

Holding and expressing one's power often requires courage and responsibility, but there is a paradox here that many find confusing: When people do not trust the expanded notion of power within the partnership paradigm (*power-with*), they may allow someone else to hold power over them by reason of apathy or culpable neglect, which devolves into tacit agreement. In this manner, the individual's inherent power is eventually co-opted, restricted, and sabotaged, and in their despair they collude in supporting a system that treats them as pawns to be played in some grand game of winner-takes-all.

One of the most entrenched examples of the win-lose paradigm of the power game occurs in the electoral system in the United States, which produces a winner-take-all result, even when it contradicts the will of the majority of voters. Within this paradigm of skewed and restrictive rules, power becomes a high-stakes game to be won at all costs. This opportunity to emerge victorious without the requirement of coalition building that occurs in other systems feeds the ambitions of those who harbor images of grandiosity, whether individually or nationally. The conquering hero and the all-powerful patriarch are important mythic images in modern American culture. In the face of terrorist threats to the American homeland, the valiant hero-patriarch has been further lionized by action-figure media images, and subsequently representatives of that persona have even been selected as "leaders" by a hopeful public with a longing for salvation by this superman under the mantle of super-power.

This power-over bravado trades on a grandiose narcissistic unconsciousness. Narcissism, as communication professors Marc Porter and Isaac Catt explain, "is the experience of an inability to distinguish the boundary or outline of the self" (167). When that condition exists, any discourse that occurs is dependent on a self that "does not have an *other* against whom to measure the lucidity of its thought" (166). In other words, within the narcissistic mindset, the importance and needs of *me* and *mine* outweigh the importance of the common good.

There is grave danger in operating in such a mono-dimensional vacuum, yet Starhawk warns, "The cult at the heart of American culture is that of personality, offering as its highest reward the narcissistic joy of Making It" (*Dreaming the Dark* 127). Those caught up in the determination to *make it* often have the sense, as Porter and Catt describe, that the "world [is] an extension of the self" (167). That sense in turn supports the presumptions that everything and everyone exists as an object, property, or *other*, which exists and is "there to be manipulated" for their own benefit (Porter and Catt 167). Furthermore, the organization or institution itself becomes, as Jungian analyst Eugene Monick observes, "their narcissism, a reflection of their standing in the world," which then when given power and control over it stands as "their legitimacy confirmed" (102). Within that framework, rampant exploitation—whether displayed by a nation intent on raiding the world's resources to feed a voracious consumer society, by department heads who blithely take credit and reward for others' efforts, or by corporate executives who raid company coffers, leaving thousands with reduced or nonexistent pension funds—becomes an operational norm. While people rail against such behavior, little is done to fix the damage.

Exploitation and discrimination are further justified by another one of the trademarks of narcissism: a belief that one's own reflection provides "the measure of what society should look like" (Porter and Catt 175). This attitude, reflected in the dictum "You can work here only if you too become like us," discourages diversity and encourages both organizational and cultural entropy. Porter and Catt confirm that narcissism "adversely affects the possibilities of creating the kind of authentic, pluralistically responsive dialogue that is the prerequisite for emancipation from organizational systems of domination" (166). The result is "communication" that is merely a façade—"a neurosis in which people only appear to be engaged in substantive dialogue" (176), and which, if anything, merely reinforces the power and domination of the in-house narcissistic heroes.

Among those personal characteristics that feed one's impulse to solidify power over others is the gross narcissism of grandiosity. This characteristic is displayed when individuals portray themselves as people who are larger-than-life—the Napoleonic delusions of grandeur, for example—or who are so unyielding in the conviction of their vision or contribution to their particular field that no one can offer countering information that might sway them from their task. As the old saying goes, "My mind is made up; don't confuse me with the facts." Some attribute this behavior to psychological pretense, including French, who declares, "The dream underlying the drive to power is transcendence: the accomplishment by humans of a godlike invincibility, impregnability, untouchableness, the ability to affect others without being affected ourselves" (510). This is the classic individual who demonstrates a self-righteous belief in his or her own innate superiority. On the other hand, Jungian analyst Allan Guggenbühl believes, "A man becomes grandiose because of the myth using him as an instrument" (105); this "true believer" dedicates his all to a cause, which he perceives simultaneously to be larger than himself and embodied by his very being. In this way, the myth eventually consumes the narcissist, or as the cliché goes, "The bigger they are the harder they fall."

Grandiosity does not always have entirely negative outcomes, although the lengths to which some people will go to achieve their transcendent goals are quite amazing. Examples include Christopher Columbus (1451-1506), who introduced himself as "Grand Admiral of the Ocean Sea" before he had even assembled a fleet (Guggenbühl 118). Galileo Galilei (1564-1642), who was so sure of his rejection of the geocentric perspective that the Inquisitors persecuted him not once, but multiple times in their efforts to dissuade him of his blasphemy, demonstrated a degree of grandiosity. Even though Galileo recanted under duress, he did not change his mind. Guggenbühl notes that Galileo felt "he could not do otherwise than think and teach what his science had revealed to him" (106). On the other hand, Adolf Hitler also exhibited an expression of grandiosity in his overarching goal of exterminating the entire Jewish population and controlling all of Europe. Grandiosity is one of those patterns that cuts both ways, prompting both exhilarating accomplishments and appalling extremism, and it is intimately related to the distribution of power in the authoritarian, *power-over* system.

When woven together, the threads of competition, narcissism, grandiosity, heroic displays of force, and reliance on reason (at the exclusion of emotional and spiritual inputs) form a *power-over* fabric that appears uncompromisingly solid, yet upon closer examination is revealed to be superficial and ephemeral. As French asserts, no one can ever get enough *power-over* to feel fully in control (507). Thus it becomes an addictive force that drives its adherents even beyond the limits of their much-vaunted reason and makes the prospect of surrendering their power, and its attendant privilege, all the more difficult. Yet such power is gained for the losing. As Starhawk observes, "The top rungs [of the ladder] are isolated and unstable. One can always fall" (*Dreaming the Dark* 127). Consequently, behind the bombastic veils of narcissism and grandiosity, some ascertain a restless discomfort and insecurity that require ever-increasing domination and control. Some individuals spend most of their lives testing and learning to re-evaluate the usefulness of *power-over* approaches:

Do you know what astonished me most in the world?
The inability of force to create anything.
In the long run, the sword is always beaten by the spirit.
&. Napoleon Bonaparte (Stated near the end of his life)

Those who have traditionally held the most *power-over* options have the most to lose. In Americentric societies, the traditional power-holders have been the white, able-bodied, attractive, heterosexual, fit, Protestant males of the upper social classes—with maleness trumping all of the other characteristics. In that respect, social theorist and philosopher Victor Jeleniewski Seidler examines the perceived need for men to prove themselves in the eyes of other men. He observes, "Within an Enlightenment vision of modernity in which masculinity can never be taken for granted but always has to be proved, the hidden question that is never far from the surface of consciousness is 'Am I man enough?'" (184). Individual efforts to assuage that anxiety vary widely, ranging from demeaning girls and women as "silly" and "emotional" or "hyper-sensitive" to controlling organizations with an iron hand, and recklessly bombing the "evildoers." To that end, Cynthia Cockburn asserts, "The anti-feminist discourse of men has to be seen as a policing of women's consciousness and an important mechanism in the reproduction of male power" (168). Any time the identity of an entire group (e.g., feminists, women in general, minorities, or non-Christian religions in an increasingly pluralistic America) can be demeaned, the rhetoric of power also reduces their chance to be heard—and to be perceived as a potential threat to the maintenance of the *power-over* status quo.

Shifting Power Valences

With the rise of feminism, Seidler allows, "The traditional gender contract has had to be renegotiated" (186). James Hillman concurs, "The feminist focus on power has shifted many of the usual valences" (*Kinds of Power* 204). As millions of women have entered the workplace in positions not previously open to them, feminism both added to the challenges for men to prove themselves in the context of independence and control, and simultaneously challenged women to re-think their own desired relationship to power. Unfortunately, those early female entrants were only allowed a place at the table when they demonstrated their ability to "take it like a man." As transpersonal psychologist Claudio Naranjo, in *The End of Patriarchy* points out, "All too commonly the early story of the women's movement was one of competition for male prerogatives in which there continued to operate that implicit 'mismeasure of women' ... according to which patriarchal standards continued to be unquestioned" (31). Surface-level changes—represented by just getting in the door—preceded the needed fundamental changes in the organizational *underground*.

Thus, in the upper echelons of management and in "nontraditional" settings, many women in the early years of the movement clamored to compete on traditional male turf by using traditionally male tactics. On the other hand, in the quest to have their voices and perspectives heard, some early women's groups went to the other extreme; they sought to value and emphasize "feminine traits" such as feeling, listening, and nurturing to the exclusion of traditionally perceived "masculine" intellectual values. Fortunately, in some arenas a deep shift is occurring. Both men and women are examining both their own inner blend of "masculine" and "feminine" traits and their relationships with others, and consciously choosing different modes of working together, which includes redefining their identities, their relationships, and the valences of power. To that end, Naranjo concedes, "The new feminism embraces an appreciation of differences and orients itself to the understanding of complementarity" (31). This is the kind of attitude and openness that encourages dialogue and the development of *power-with* relationships.

The *power-over* system of domination and control has for too long been presented as the only viable system of managing power. Within that paradigm, the goal of power is presented as monolithic and wielding overwhelming force. Eminent psychiatrist David Hawkins in *Power vs. Force* explains that in accordance with the laws of physics, force (which corresponds to *power-over*) "automatically creates counter-force" and "is incomplete and therefore has to be fed energy constantly" (132). Furthermore, he notes the "effect of force [*power-over*] is to polarize rather than unify. Polarization always implies conflict; its cost, therefore, is always high." He continues, "It inevitably produces a win/lose dichotomy . . . and requires a constant defense" (133). Supplying counter-force and maintaining defensiveness is a costly drain of both energy and power in any relationship, at any level.

Applying *power-with* principles to relationships has the effect of unleashing energy that had been bound by the strict controls instituted in traditional systems. The application process starts with recognition of additional sources of power, which is necessary in order to effectively use and integrate *power-with* in the partnership paradigm. For example, just as there is great power in the tiny seedling or in small slivers of frozen water that force apart great boulders, and in the slow inexorable force of tides and plate tectonics, there is power in information, in connection, in empathetically and lovingly witnessing another's pain. Starhawk notes, "The word 'power' comes from a root that means 'ability.'" Thus, she reasons, "We each have a different kind of power: the power that comes from within; our ability to dare, to do, and to dream; our creativity" (*Webs of Power* 6). Hawkins suggests, "Power [which in his lexicon corresponds to *power-with*] arises from *meaning*, and has to do with motive and principle." In that respect, he contends, "Power is always associated with that which supports the significance of life itself...is total and complete in itself, and requires nothing from the outside." Consequently, rather than the energy drain required to maintain force/*power-over*, power/*power-with* is an energy generator.

At the core of every variant in the movements to reclaim "rights" and subvert systemic domination is the hunger to have a sense of influence over one's own dignity and destiny. That hunger fuels efforts that arise in the face of formidable obstacles—and thus hunger itself is power. This is part of the paradox that is often confusing, both for those who think they can control so-called powerless groups and for those who retreat into victim-hood, nursing unrequited hunger.

It is difficult to imagine operating from a completely different power paradigm—let alone know where to begin. Starhawk concedes, "The implications are radical and far-reaching, because all of our present institutions, from the most oppressive to the most benign, are based on the authority some individuals hold that allows them to control others" (*Dreaming the Dark* 12). Yet the shift in the power equilibrium lies at the crux of the move beyond the *power-over* system of competition, domination, and control. As Cockburn emphasizes, "The way we understand power is the way we understand society, and to use power differently is to create a different world" (241). The radical notion of fundamentally redefining power dynamics is an intimidation to those with low tolerance for ambiguity, and an even bigger threat for those who have a vested interest in maintaining the status quo.

Yet even for those who understand the differences in power dynamics and want to make the shift, the way is not always clear. Hillman nails the core question by asking how we can collectively "act without dominion, without oppressive control, and yet accomplish?" (*Kinds of Power* 98). Admittedly, it takes an enormous amount of energy, dedication, and hard work to accomplish an organizational culture shift away from competitive groups, as the people of the NEFA agency express in chapter 5. Nevertheless, they also witnessed and are experiencing the benefits of having broken through the inertia of the old system and dramatically shifted along the continuum in the direction of *power-with*.

Rather than isolated independence, theirs is a model of *inter*dependence, where everyone recognizes that their success (or failure) depends on the whole, not just their piece or "turf." They have approached the model that Buddhists have long called *dependent co-arising*, which quite simply means operating based on the knowledge that everything is connected to everything else (Golden, Macy, and Brown). In this circumstance, interdependence is consistent with what Naranjo calls *complementarity*, meaning that by integrating different perspectives and talents we contribute to a greater whole. The deep understanding of that interdependence is itself a good beginning point for the move toward a partnership organization.

This hunger-power-from-within was also quite effectively tapped by the simple teachings of the Brazilian priest, Paolo Freire, whose classic book *Pedagogy of the Oppressed* was recently published in a thirtieth anniversary edition. His concepts of "concientización" encompass the notion of liberation as a mutual effort, which begins with each individual. Through his revolutionary pedagogy, Freire opened the minds and hearts of poor Latin American peasants, and taught them that they *could* make a difference in the lives they and their families experienced. His legacy lives to this day in Brazilian communities such as Salvador, in the state of Bahia, where many local groups have collectively transformed their living conditions, and whose mayor recently offered to host the next (post-Beijing) United Nations International Conference of Women.

Those Brazilian groups inspired and taught by Freire have continued his legacy by demonstrating the powerful potential that is unleashed when individuals experience that, as Starhawk observes, "Power-from-within encompasses the power to change ourselves" (*Dreaming* 122). When we exercise courage and take the steps to change ourselves, then she believes, "Reclaiming personal power gives us the courage to demand a change in the basis of society's power" (*Dreaming* 71). Publicizing success stories of individuals and groups who have stepped through their fears and uncertainty and realized their goals often gives others the courage to step up and claim their own power. That spreading of courageous dissent is also the reason there is such a concerted effort by those in control of the *power-over* system to control access to all media outlets—in order to stifle and suppress those stories— and why it is equally important to keep those channels open and accessible by all.

An organization that is sincerely examining its power basis along with its mission, structure, norms, and culture will find that by supporting individuals in their quest to express their personal *power-from-within*, there is in effect a new power source available to the collective itself. Unlike those who vie for the tyranny of absolute equality, when people are treated with dignity and respect, and recognized as valued members of the group, they do not have to have equality in every last detail in order to experience a sense of *power-with*. They can relax the constant striving to prove themselves and to win, even from winning at equality. The energy they would have expended in trying to wrest some sense of dignity and ability to affect their lives and to be treated fairly can then be released for the greater work and benefit of the whole.

Within a *power-with* partnership organization, opportunities for learning and expanding one's skills are encouraged and supported, with recognition that when one person expands what they have to offer and is supported in sharing their offerings, the entire entity benefits. This has been one of the underlying strengths of the NEFA Agency; when organizational members are able to clearly state their desire for further training or education and make the link in how it will improve their abilities to contribute to the organization, the agency leader Sophia will do everything in her capacity to support their quest, and many have undertaken difficult courses of study that have indeed benefited the organization.

Within a partnership organization, communication and teamwork are not taken for granted or dismissed as "touchy-feely;" they are valued, taught, and modeled by group leaders. In a group where everyone is considered a leader, that means everyone shares the responsibility—and power—to make sure that communication is open and forthright and that teams are truly operating as teams, and not as loosely confederated groups or collectives, fiercely preoccupied with protecting turf. Everyone is clearly aware that they participate in creating a *power-with* environment by practicing facilitative behavior in every meeting and every interaction, whether internally or externally. Facilitative behavior involves both self and group monitoring to be sure that no one person dominates the "air time" in meetings, that everyone has a chance to be heard and contribute, that the conversation stays on track and is not allowed to wander and waste valuable time, that there is a climate of mutual trust and respect, and that disagreements are aired without resorting to personal attacks.

Finally, the organizational "bottom line" becomes focused on finding ways to both maintain profits and operate sustainably, thereby taking care of both people and the earth, with consideration given to the well being of following generations. There are emerging examples of successful businesses that operate based on these principles, such as Patagonia, which is a company that prides itself on its "good humor and brilliant service" and was one of the early providers of on-site childcare and recycling, while providing admirable support for employees and quality products created with integrity.

Is this notion of organizations operating on the basis of *power-with* systems some simplistic, pie–in–the–sky concept, or is there solid evidence that it works? The organizational partnership examples given in chapter 5 encompass varying degrees of *power-with* among their employees; they demonstrate that it can work and be effective in creating and sustaining highly successful organizations.

There is a growing awareness of the damage that continues to be done under the relentless micro-management of *power-over* practitioners, and there are concurrently growing numbers of people who are talking, writing, and working toward *power-with* organizational alternatives. To that end, Starhawk calls for "a revolution that changes the very nature of how power is structured and perceived, that challenges *all* systems of domination and control, that nurtures the empowerment of individuals and the collective power we can wield when we act together in solidarity" (*Webs of Power* 96). Her call applies to both local organizations and to the global scale, where Starhawk and others hope that the synergy of their actions against the World Trade Organization (WTO), the World Bank, the North American Free Trade Area (NAFTA), and the Free Trade Area of the Americas (FTAA) will indeed help to shift the valences of power away from mega-corporate interests to favoring the common people and the conservation of the earth's resources, for the benefit of all humanity. At the very least they are drawing attention to the widely destructive practices of powerful multi- and trans-national corporations, led by those who seem driven to dominate global economies and their related socio-political systems, and to author the lives of more people than any ancient conqueror could have imagined.

Meanwhile, millions of *Cultural Creatives* are participating in localized power shifts that involve their workplaces, their communities, their governing bodies, and their interpersonal relationships. Their initiatives often start at the most basic levels.

They are weaving conscious webs of inclusion that employ complex, flexible connections, starting with simple suggestions for changing the way the myriad of meetings are run that occur everyday in organizations around the country. To that end, Mike, the Administrative Assistant in a mid-sized manufacturing firm, was the initial promoter of new meetings management tools that encountered stiff resistance at the outset, and have since become "standard operating procedure" appreciated by all meeting attendees.

They are encouraging and participating in dialogues about the norms, or standards of behavior that are expected within the organization, and making the power dynamics consciously explicit. Brenda, a new project manager at a Fortune 500 company, used the occasion of her Transition Meeting to open the dialogue about group norms, and to establish the foundation for a new climate for that sector of the organization.

They are going beyond "valuing diversity" with token ethnic food luncheons and canned, mandatory trainings by engaging in in-depth training sessions that weave together intercultural communication skills, understanding of cultural conflict styles, and dialogues that seek to identify ways of working together that respect differences and incorporate an ethic of service. In that respect, Sybil, the Vice-President of Sales in a family-owned business that is expanding into the global marketplace, led the movement from "gaining cooperation"—which relies on charisma, persuasion, and/or coercion—to "How can I help you?"—an approach that reflects a tolerance for ambiguity and multiplicity, and invites respect while providing service. She was able to overcome a general distrust regarding communication training and an expectation that everyone "should be like Americans" if they want to do business here, and open an on-going series of conversations that address questions about how to incorporate partnership principles in an increasingly diverse business arena.

They are seeking, as did Susan, the long-time secretary for a private school, to reframe destructive *underground* conflicts that had been festering for years, and thereby promote new understandings of differences that include holding conflicts as learning opportunities—and then being sure to *facilitate* the learning—and to incorporate new ways of negotiating understanding relationships and collectively seeking common ground.

All of these connections in turn acknowledge that power is energy, and that *power-with* synergy unleashes surprising amounts of energy that had previously been captured and suspended by those who wielded *power-over* control. Within these relationship webs—often aided these days by the electronic World Wide Web—we discover unconventional ways in which people are recognizing, holding, and managing power, while demonstrating an organic model of leadership that co-creates and shapes innovative organizational containers and invites active and responsible participation from everyone in the organization.

Powerful Partnerships in the Common Ground

Contributed by W. Marc Porter, PhD

One approach for creating partnerships is revealed in Marc Porter's *Common Ground Model*. Porter, an organizational development (OD) consultant, this book's editor, and the author of this section, developed the model nearly 20 years ago to address the ethics of interventions by management consultants. He observed that when OD consultants spoke about their professional ethics, they habitually pointed at issues surrounding confidentiality, doing no harm, and knowing your client—which was always the one paying the bill. Consultants, in this vein, were not partners in organizational change, but more like extra hands and heads to help management—which meant the *power-over* structure was not to be touched. Their role was more akin to an attorney responsible for advocating a client's position, as opposed to taking the role of peacemaker seeking to help different parties (not just one person) create and sustain partnerships. In contrast, the *Common Ground Model* suggests that partnership grows when one understands the relational and communicative nature of how people get along at work. Thus, the *Common Ground Model* reframes "client," not as management or employees, but rather as the conversation between and among people in the organization.

The *Common Ground Model*, consistent with creating the partnership organization, tackles head on systems of domination and control by understanding the communicative nature of conflict in the organization and recognizing that partnership by definition requires at least two parties. As obvious as the observation may be that an individual cannot be a partner with oneself, many models for creating participative organizational culture are based in individualistic psychologies, particularly behavioral psychology. The *Common Ground Model*, like the *Partnership Model*, is not a psychological perspective; it is a communicative one. Communication is fundamentally about balancing our need for creativity and relational expression with our needs for coordination. Patriarchal rules emphasize control and presume that absolute clarity is possible in any message to employees. The partnership organization holds that clarity (fidelity) and mystery (ambiguity) are always present in equal measure, and it is through coordination among people that we find dynamic balance between creativity and structure. The *Common Ground Model* reflects this partnership perspective by recognizing that progress is a shared journey and that *common ground* is forever in a state of transformation and flux.

The *Common Ground Model* recasts how people experience "progress" in an organization, by suggesting that progress is something subjective, something much more than technical mastery and invention. For example, when work is not going well, people describe the organization as "not progressing." On the other hand, when people at work feel truly included in the system, engaged in sharing power, and proud of their unique place, they will describe the organization as "progressive." The word "progress" is used instead of "time" to make clear the subjective sense of advancement people feel as events move at glacier or light speeds.

The *Common Ground Model* also tackles a common sense notion of conflict that assumes "some conflict is good." This taken-for-granted notion begs the question: How much conflict is good? The answer may be arbitrary, but from one organizational culture to the next it is rarely capricious. The general answer is that conflict is bad when it begins to attack people's core beliefs and values and demonstrates gross disrespect and incivility. Where that line is crossed from "good conflict" to "bad conflict" is a matter of perception among organizational members.

Turn the assertion around, then to consider: If some conflict is good, is too little conflict bad? Most conflict resolution models focus on "bad conflict" being only the highly intense battles between two parties, and few consider how entropy can become equally destructive because two parties becoming increasingly non-communicative in the effort to avoid conflict. Thus, in the *underground*, people stop talking to each other about what really matters, what's bugging them, and then act in ways that denies the existence of conflict. Groupthink is certainly one result of nominal conflict; parties refuse to criticize decisions and avoid conflict to such an extent that individual perspectives and even critical information may be withheld, and riskier decisions are ultimately made.

In the *Common Ground Model*, the *battleground* refers to the zone where intense value conflict resides or erupts with high levels of *intensity*, so high it exceeds either or both parties' ability to cope because they are consumed with winning at any cost, fearful that loss means their own demise. People caught in the *battleground* feel their position and character threatened, often become defensive, and may withdraw. When the intensity drops dramatically between the parties, the disagreement or conflict does not go away, but moves into the shadow aspect of the organization, where it resembles more of a loosely held tug-of-war rope, and it is called the *underground*. The *underground* retards civility because it avoids honest discourse. People hide in the *underground* because they feel that confronting the real issues with others will result only in a major battle. Unfortunately, few people are prepared or able to cope with a perceived conflict or "battle" situation in any way other than either confrontation or avoidance: fight or flight. Indeed, many individuals share the assumption that those are the only choices.

In many respects, one can liken this tension to what occurs in the majority of failed marriages in which the couple did not argue about anything before calling it quits. They may have attended dinner parties with friends, and few, if any, suspected that under the surface real differences were taking root. The divorce may appear sudden and unexpected to friends, family or even their children because people did not see the stereotypical soap opera in which the couple argue with increasing volume and frequency. While not as entertaining as television drama, many relationships die in the *underground*, suffocated by deafening silence. The erosion of the relationship in the *underground* relies on denial and culpable neglect. The eventual dissolution thus results from long-term wearing down that unravels the fabric to such an extent it can no longer hold.

There is an alternative. The *common ground* emerges between the *battleground* and *underground*. It is the place where civility, respect, acceptance of ambiguity, tolerance for conflict, and thus true partnership find greatest expression. The *common ground* is not a static zone between the other two, but rather its boundaries are permeable and fluid, and therefore they shrink and swell over time as they shift and are impacted by the complex nature of human relationships. An organization can at the outset have only a thin line where commonality is found, yet with serious work, the people in that organization can consciously and collectively grow the *common ground*. Spreading the boundaries of the *common ground*, or inversely shrinking the *battleground* and the *underground*, requires that the people in the organization must develop their collective ability to work from a place of civility and respect, to appreciate that ambiguity is a part of life and essential to creativity and freedom, and to tolerate a greater range of conflict without allowing it to explode into value attacks or sink into passive-aggressive avoidance or guerrilla-inspired sabotage.

Central to growing the *common ground* is the ability of people to attend consciously to the conversation already in progress. The *common ground* grows not by eliminating intensity of conflicts, nor by seeking ways to move as quickly as possible into the *common ground* in order to achieve a sense of stability and comfort, but rather by acknowledging that mature human relationships involve broadening our ability to manage that intensity while honestly seeking a sense of mutual understanding—whether or not all parties agree on all points. Whether as external OD consultants, counselors, or leaders, our work is not to take up sides in the tug-of-war; rather it is to encourage dismantling the tug-of-war and to help the parties find a way through their conflicts and leverage their differences, not as a source of divisiveness and competition, but rather as something inherently human that ultimately broadens shared perspectives, brings forth critical information, and benefits the creation of partnerships.

Take a classic problem in which management calls in an expert to convince employees that productivity is down and must be increased. The consultant spends time with employees and learns from them that productivity is down because quality of work life is abysmal. Employees argue that productivity will go up when quality of work life is improved; management counters that quality of work life will be addressed when productivity increases. Eventually, the tug-of-war can lead to *battleground* tactics—like union strikes and punitive management policies and practices. Quite often, the struggle will find an uneasy stasis in the *underground*, whereby productivity will not increase significantly and quality of work life may amount to token appeasement, such as a new microwave in the break room. The problem is not that management is right and employees wrong (or vice versa), but rather that they have talked themselves into a mutually exclusive dichotomy. Productivity and quality of work life are not inherent opposites, but as is the nature of commonly held views of human conflicts, they become such in the workplace. The consultant's role is not to choose the winning side of this tug-of-war, but rather to help the parties open new channels of communication, which support figuring out a solution for themselves. That means helping them negotiate a path out of the *underground,* and possibly through some difficult time in the *battleground,* before making possible their ability to work collaboratively again in the *common ground.*

Throughout this book it is emphasized that creating partnership organizations is not a Pollyanna approach, meaning that no organization is completely free of conflict and filled only with people who adore one another no matter what. A partnership organization navigates conflicts quite differently than a power-over organization. Central to the *Common Ground Model* is the premise that civility expands to the degree that people find ways to increase their tolerance for conflict and ambiguity. Trust in this context is a relational characteristic, not an individual matter of style. While people may not all "just get along," organizations operating in the *common ground* have a greater degree of openness, acceptance, and skill for working through conflicts.

This is not to say that every conflict at work is fully resolved, but rather that they are managed, and not buried or used as bludgeons. People consciously work through differences, even if that means taking "time outs" when resolution may not be clear. When conflicts explode beyond a group's capacity to talk to one another or to call upon others to help them tackle the escalating differences before they explode, the organization rolls into the *battleground*. I have worked with a variety of companies to help them eradicate workplace discrimination and create more respectful workplaces. It was in these settings that the *Common Ground Model* became increasingly useful for tracking the organizational progress from a highly divisive place into one in which people with very different perspectives and experiences could work collaboratively. A company's request for a "multicultural intervention" more often than not came when it was facing rising harassment claims, and possibly had received an imposed consent degree to "fix it." In other words, the organization was already in the *battleground*, where parties were tugging hard at their end of the rope in order to destroy the other's resistance as a means of achieving their goals. Typically, after a few months of work involving "respect in the workplace" programs, things would appear to calm down. Yet, employees in highly distrustful workplaces are not fools, and they realize that once battles are won or lost, the hierarchy once again sustains *power-over*. In that case, they perceive that their best bet is to hide in the *underground* until they can secure a better position from which to attack at another time. In that case, when asked about how things were going since the multicultural awareness workshops, employees often say, "No conflicts here." "We're doing fine." "Really am glad we got that stuff behind us." "Glad we did it, not sure it was enough, but then not sure how much else we could really do." "Hey, I'm just trying to get along and keep my job."

When people feel that the *power-over* structure, with its emphasis on domination and control, is too overwhelming to challenge, they hide their feelings and allow animosities to fester in the *underground*. They realize that it is dangerous to make a direct attack on the hierarchy from a subordinate position. Insubordination remains one of the most common reasons for termination, and it smacks entirely of those who challenged, for whatever reason, the prevailing way of doing things to such an extent that the people in positions of power "pull rank." Insubordination is by definition a direct challenge to the *power-over* structure, the legitimate power in the patriarchal organization. In that respect, many organizations operate for most of their existences with very little *common ground*. In other words, only a narrow band of civility may exist in such organizations; those without power hide, and those with position power make it clear they will use it if challenged. The dictatorship—whether autocratic or benevolent—is alive and well in many corporations, and represents the poster child of patriarchal systems.

The *Common Ground Model* makes clear that in order for people to find progress in their work, they must work consciously to expand their capacity to tolerate both ambiguity and conflict, and develop their ability to deal directly with differences. When people lack information (e.g., about their job expectations, about a potential downsizing, or about the health of a co-worker), they will fill in the void with all kinds of conjecture. These inferences can run amuck, fuel the rumor mill, and become quickly not fiction, but held as absolute truths in organizations with thin *common grounds* and widening *battlegrounds* and *undergrounds*.

Growing the *common ground* means making it safe and normal to check regularly our perceptions and assumptions, and to challenge openly and empathetically someone's interpretation without dismissing or threatening the person or group. For example, during one multicultural workshop, an older white male supervisor asked, "So why is it offensive to call certain people 'Orientals,' for I thought all my life that that was showing respect?" Because little *common ground* existed yet in that organization, the innocent question was interpreted as discriminatory and insensitive. Even though the question was asked and later answered honestly, and the flashpoint of tensions was relieved, conflict seethed among folks from that session for weeks, and rumors circulated that a grievance would be filed, and this offered as more evidence of an insensitive culture. Over several months, as employees continued to understand and to expand their sense of *common ground*, that same question could have been asked without fear of derision, and would be interpreted by others not as a personal attack, but as an opportunity to move through a conflict and make stronger their *common ground*. In contrast, a senior male executive posed a similar kind of question: "What if the ladies in my office aren't offended if I call them 'girls'?" Because the tolerance for conflict and for sincere, shared exploration was far greater, as a result of months of work to build *common ground*, the question did not trigger World War III in the office, but rather resulted in a solid conversation that no longer needed an external facilitator to mediate. In this case, the person who spoke to the senior leader was herself several ranks below him. They resolved it without a grievance filed, a shot fired, or a bunker dug. Moreover, their ability to move through the conflict fueled a greater sense of partnership, for stories like this one are told and retold throughout the organization as all employees contribute to writing the organizational myths of what is and is not possible, is and is not acceptable.

The *Common Ground Model* does not promote the notion that organizations will always operate in the *common ground*, for that's not realistic. Rather, the model provides a map for how over time an organization can move in and out of conflicts in constructive or destructive ways. For example, on those occasions when we have been called in to "head off" a harassment problem, we had to be clear with the client that in all likelihood the problems were buried in the *underground* and that the act of talking about them would likely bring them out into the open and thus send them into the *battleground*. Our skills required helping them negotiate through uncomfortable parts of this journey from *underground* to *battleground* and hopefully into *common ground*. They also had to acknowledge that because of a history of neglecting themselves and each other, the *common ground* would be nearly nonexistent, but it could be restored and "grown" by conscious tending.

In that respect, many corporations that launched multicultural interventions or (more recently) "diversity and inclusion" initiatives were aghast to find that once issues were put on the table instead of seeing a decline in grievances, they witnessed their rise. No wonder some managers wanted to "get back to the way things were," for the journey through the uncharted, transitional *wilderness* now required that people genuinely address (or otherwise legally resolve) discrimination complaints. Organizational leaders faced the choice to grow the *common ground* or simply allow hostilities to return to the *underground*—where progress becomes only an illusion. When the *common ground* becomes the goal, the path to creating truer, sustainable partnership is possible.

Many believe that participative leadership is more costly because it is more time-consuming than the wickedly efficient autocratic style. This assumption is wrong. The *Common Ground Model* emphasizes taking the longer view that progress is more clearly expressed and attained when we work consciously toward succeeding both individually and collectively, instead of wasting time figuring out how to control or destroy the other party. It is the competitive impulse to attack and defend or to control and conquer that is far more inefficient and short-sided. The partnership organization rests on the assertion that human relationships are complex, and that differences contribute to the richness of our experiences together. Indeed, partnerships, meaning relationships with conscious integrity, do not feign being colorblind or gender neutral, for those delusions perpetuate a false sense of equality. Rather, partnerships flourish when differences are acknowledged, not masked, and when unique experiences complement collaborative action, rather than attempt to disguise a consultative decision as something issuing from the whole team.

Work at a large telecommunications company demonstrates how an entire division can move from relatively volatile conflicts toward *common ground* and experience higher productivity through powerful collaborative work. From its inception through its first 10-months, employees were asked one question: "On a scale of one to ten, with 1 being *high battleground* or *high underground* and 10 being *high common ground*, where do you think we are?" The question was simple enough to ask at any meeting. The average in the first two months was

4—and through more inquiry, the *underground* was perceived to have the advantage. Occasionally, employees were asked, "What percentages of time are you spending in the *battleground*, *common ground*, and *underground*?" And the follow-up question would be, "If we are successful over the next few months in growing the *common ground*, what do you realistically expect those percentages to look like?" By year's end, the average had moved from a 4 to an 8, and the reported percentage of time spent in the *common ground* doubled. So what happen to make that shift?

At the end of the previous year, company leaders after reviewing employee satisfaction surveys and hearing about the costs of turnover and absenteeism demanded that supervisors be held accountable for how well their employees perceived their boss and how satisfied they were with the company. One division of the company with particularly low scores asked for outside help. An internal cross-functional team was formed to consider the survey findings and the charge from corporate leaders. The *Common Ground Model* was introduced, and the team adopted a slogan "Grow the Green." Green meant the organizational commons, as in a grassy area. The *battleground* was depicted in red, and the *underground* in brown. The vice-president who ran the division called for a one-day retreat to ensure support from his division's senior directors. Not all directors supported the effort or would be convinced that a transformation was possible; several felt more comfortable holding fast to the bureaucratic mindset learned in their early days when the company operated as a monopoly. But the industry was changing, and the division leader recognized that innovation would come through greater collaboration, not less.

While reluctant participants looked on, several cross-functional teams emerged to confront real issues in the division while applying the concepts of the *Common Ground*

Model. Anyone who has participated in a large move from one office building to another knows how territorial disputes can quickly divide even a fairly civil workgroup. In this case, a team was formed to look at office assignments in the new building; an older director initially assigned the task refused to work with the team, even though he was told to assist them. When the relocation of more than 200 people occurred, satisfaction levels across this division actually increased, and several senior corporate leaders remarked that this was the smoothest move they had witnessed in the company's history.

Other teams tackled coordination problems and streamlined hand-offs. Two teams worked to refine different elements of their division's marketing plans, which they had heard rumor where under review, but no one knew who was authoring new marketing strategies, where they were in the process, and what they were addressing—and no one would tell them. All the teams operated with the full support of the division leader, and were supported by two OD specialists (including one external consultant). Each team chose its own leader, and met at least monthly to work on its project. In one case, administrative assistants and secretaries frustrated with the endless number of complex forms asked to form an "action team." Their work resulted in an internal website that identified who knew best how to complete particular forms, with examples of properly completed forms available on a shared server. About a month after this solution was launched, training and development specialists arrived from the corporate offices, addressed the internal OD consultant and division vice-president, and explained that they had been in the process of designing a series of courses on how to fill out the myriad forms. Apparently, the T&D group had not told any of those who might be affected by the training about their needs analysis or their training solution. The solution developed by the secretaries remained in place because it was far more cost-effective and qualitatively better at reducing form errors than sending the people offsite for training.

As successes mounted, employees called for a "greenhouse meeting" to be held at year's end to celebrate their accomplishments. The productivity of the entire division had increased, and those increases were higher than other divisions. So successful had this effort to "grow the green" become, that corporate leaders asked for a full accounting of what happened and how much it had cost. The response surprised them. It cost the company about $1 million at "full burden rate"—meaning the cost of employees' time in meetings, plus the full-time salary of the internal OD consultant, the cost for the external consultant, the salary of one full-time assistant, and miscellaneous expenses. Costs had been tracked throughout the process. Indeed, one of those expenses difficult at first to justify was a team's request for a building-wide coffee break to be held once a month so that people could learn where others were in the new office building. Honestly, neither OD specialist was convinced this request would be accepted, and believed that it would simply go down as an expense, but they also trusted the process, and believed that more would be lost in denying the request. The doughnuts and muffins ticked off close to $1,000 for these 15-minute building-wide breaks. But several solutions emerged as a result of these building-wide breaks, including the one that brought secretaries together from across the building; the idea emerged initially at one of these office-wide coffee breaks as a result of exchanging "horror stories" about complex report forms.

For that $1 million effort to grow the *common ground* and make possible greater collaboration across the company, the organization realized over $20 million in returns, which was a conservative estimate verified by the company's chief financial officer. Return on investment examined four elements: *revenue generation*, *cost-avoidance*, *cost-savings*, and *climate/culture change.*

Revenue generation is by far the most convincing measure to most corporate leaders because it shows how an innovation increased the amount of money the company made. Several projects, all identified by cross-functional teams committed to growing the *common ground* and operating in partnership, returned major gains to the division, mostly because the teams were better able to examine and address customer concerns more effectively than traditional methods that rely on silo decision-making structures.

Cost-avoidance is the second strongest component for it looks at what the company had predicted to lose and demonstrated how improvements reduced or eliminated that cost. Reducing unwanted turnover is one solid example of cost-avoidance, and it was in this case as well. Reducing errors on forms was another example.

Cost-savings are important, but they are not always convincing. For instance, the company spent $3 million on one marketing plan, whereas this effort required $1 million, and resulted in numerous marketing strategy adjustments and a modest marketing plan. One could say then that "$2 million was saved," but it begs the question as to whether the less expensive solution was qualitatively as good as the more expensive one. In this case, surveys showed that after nine months 86% of the division's employees could articulate both key elements of the marketing plan (meaning the one they had participating in designing) and their role in its execution. In contrast, the more expensive plan was rolled out for review after nine months, and until then had been seen by only five senior leaders and a couple of top-tier consultants. Within a month this latter marketing plan was under scrutiny because it had overlooked numerous variables and required a multi-million dollar investment risk unexpected by several corporate leaders who had not been involved in the process. The more costly marketing plan was not scratched, but it was shelved for reconsideration. In contrast, marketing ideas implemented through collaborative action teams working in partnership across functions were already yielding significant results, for employees from the cross-functional teams had anticipated and addressed many of the most pressing issues for customers. In other words, while cost-savings may not be singularly persuasive, it was worth noting.

Lastly, *organizational climate* measures told us if we had harmed or improved the culture. In fact, measures of trust, participation in decision-making, high performance, and job satisfaction increased significantly. Even though this metric does not demonstrate a direct financial impact to the company, it is important to track and report. The effort originally began over concerns with low job satisfaction. Moreover, if "growing the *common ground*" was to mean something to employees beyond simply a slogan, then it was important to know if people genuinely perceived improvements and experienced true progress in their work. In this case they did. Together these four measures provide convincing evidence that growing the *common ground* and thus developing people's ability to work collaboratively toward a partnership organization hold countless advantages for the organization. Similar results in other organizations support the notion that moving toward *power-with* organizational dynamics offers significant benefits, both for the organization as a whole and for its constituents.

ᴄᴋ Chapter 4 ᴋᴏ

Leadership in a Partnership Context

Leadership within a partnership organization is very different from the authoritarian, top-down, micro-management style of patriarchal executives, or even the benevolent style of more consultative leaders. Leadership consultants Warren Bennis and Burt Namus, in *Leaders: Strategies for Taking Charge,* offer a straightforward and often cited distinction between managing and leading that contributes to understanding the partnering style of leadership described in this chapter. They believe that managers focus on doing things "right," like meticulously implementing prescribed policies and procedures, and obsessively pursuing an action plan to its completion even when new information would indicate a change of course is needed. Leaders, on the other hand, focus on doing the "right things," which may involve mid-course corrections. Those "right things" to do for *partnering leaders* include *co-creating* (rather than imposing) the organization's vision; helping others make interconnections between vision, goals, and actions; collaboratively crafting and sustaining the organization's core values; linking those shared values to fluid and practical organizational norms; and facilitating conversations across the organization to help member-partners clarify, refine, and apply the organization's mission, or reason for being.

To be sure, there are situations that require the distinctly functional and technical skills of management, although there is lingering confusion and distortion of leadership principles within management contexts. Even the popular "Situational Leadership" model posited by organizational behavioral scientists Paul Hersey and Ken Blanchard has been *used* both by those who sincerely want to support and advance their employees in the most appropriate ways and *abused* by those who seek to control employees' access to promotional opportunities by autonomous determination of their levels of "maturity." This kind of manipulation of the model confirms the belief that a behavioralistic leadership theory alone— whether Situational Leadership, Managerial Grid, or a host of others—is not enough to affect a fundamental culture shift within the organization, and that the best of intentions can be co-opted by managers imbued with the *power-over* philosophy and approach to supervision. *Power-over* supervision involves maintaining psychological distance from subordinates in order to better impose their will.

The basic approach to both managing and leading shifts dramatically within a partnership organization from one of command and control (which presumes an exclusive, privileged position "above" others) to one based on a supportive and inclusive web of relationships that encourage dialogue and collaborative problem solving. This approach is more akin to how we currently conceive of knowledge management structures. Knowledge management systems work best when information is spread or networked across the organization rather than held by tightly controlling gatekeepers. Through a continuous process of shared discovery new connections are made and new patterns for the practical and innovative application of that knowledge are designed. Similarly, whereas traditional management skills required the ability to work systematically to a pre-determined, carefully controlled outcome, in partnership organizations the most valued skill is the ability to conceptually, flexibly, and yet systemically work through a process—perhaps without a specific, predetermined outcome—following the threads wherever they may lead, and knowing when "good enough" is sufficient for recommending action to the organization.

The leader or manager of a partnership organization is neither an all-powerful boss nor another cog in the machine, but a human being who is fully engaged in the processes and shares in the interpretation of new information, then sharing it with others in order for them both to learn from and grow into their collective knowledge. The *partnering leader* evolves beyond the preoccupation with specialization that has for so long dominated organizational theory. In today's globally interdependent and rapidly changing economies, it is evident that no specialist can stand alone. Indeed, it is the relationship of one specialized source of information to many others that provides the flexibility, depth, and adaptability necessary for organizations to move toward nurturing talent and innovation while continuing to sustain and support the organization's mission and goals.

Leader as Partner

Partnering leaders ensure that as the process of innovation unfolds (as new information feeds new knowledge, understanding, and advances):

(1) **The value of people and their unique contributions is enhanced**. Rather than receiving lip service and token awards, individuals have the opportunity to engage in dialogues that seek out and examine key questions, ask for constructive criticism (which is fundamentally different than complaining), and develop innovative proposals that although not guaranteed acceptance, are guaranteed consideration.

(2) **A culture of genuine civility and respect is established**, which supports collaboration. An organization's potential for creating viable and

genuine partnership is directly related to the health of the relationships among its employees. Such an organization is based on emerging models of leadership that emphasize inclusivity in decision-making, and civility in relationships (meaning those based on dignity, respect, trust, and concern for both personal and organizational growth). In order for true dialogue to occur, there must be a sense of safety to "speak the unspeakable," to question standard operating procedures, and to disagree with those "in charge." At the outset, the consistent use of meeting agreements and open agenda-setting processes sets the stage for developing this kind of dialogue-based organizational culture. As management professor and organizational consultant Margaret Wheatley observes in *Leadership and the New Science*, "Leadership, an amorphous phenomenon that has intrigued us since people began organizing, is being examined now for its relationship aspects" (13).

Since partnership is based on relationships, this aspect of the leadership evolution within partnership organizations is critical, and is evidenced by actions such as co-creating organizational values statements, and then making them "real" by weaving them into performance evaluation processes. Other specific actions outlined by Joan, the leader mentioned earlier who promotes partnership principles at a large food and beverage processing company, include the "four elements of leadership: listening with your full attention, showing your appreciation by thanking people, focusing on looking for the good in others, and having a sense of humor, while recognizing that work can involve a lot of stress and fear."

(3) **Innovation itself is both encouraged and understood to be an on-going process** that requires constant new information and the introduction of processes that may represent breaking the mold of revered organizational traditions. An organization will not foster true innovation if employees are constrained by outmoded information systems, restrictive "silo" communication channels, and blind adherence to sacred organizational traditions.

This leadership style replaces the model characterized by a cacophony of competition and control. In the partnership organization, there is no longer a place for cavalier risk-takers preoccupied with their own efforts for strategized advancement above all others. These are the individuals who are primarily concerned with their own quest to move up the hierarchy, and are only temporarily satisfied when their addiction to self-aggrandizement is recognized by one higher up on this rickety career ladder. In their place, the partnership organization engages those who are both heroic risk-takers *and* capable collaborators.

One of the most important reasons that American corporations have been fixated on having a strong, powerful chief executive is that it resonates with the hero myth, which incorporates the intrepid young hero and the established master or patriarch of the situation as flip sides of the same archetypal coin. This *story* reflects our need for an icon of an individual capable of slaying the dragons of competition and marshalling the troops to press on into new markets and conquer new frontiers.

Thus, when people enter an organization, they bring their own "stories" of who they are (e.g., hero, victim, power behind the throne, or king/patriarch), and what to expect (e.g., to win, to usurp, to overthrow, to be victimized). They proceed to "size-up" those they encounter in the organization, weighing in with who will support them, sabotage them, defeat them, or promote them. Sometimes they dance in sync, and sometimes they step on each other's toes, or even resort to backstabbing. Either way, as long as they are unconsciously operating based on hero-patriarch relationships with correlating expectations to be fulfilled, then the chance for success in true partnership is relatively small. Indeed, the competitive environment of the typical corporation can leave people at work fragmented, anxious, divided, and thus conquered.

The seeds of emerging partnership organizations will not take root until those willing to serve as partner-members and partner-leaders dedicate time and take action to redefine how they will work together and achieve progress together.

Partnership organizations will not be borne of a singular hero-leader charging ahead to save the day for the rest of us. Organizational researchers and consultants Fred Kofman and Peter Senge warn, "While we wait for the great leader who will save the day, we surrender the confidence and power needed to make progress" (34). On the other hand, there are some leaders busily promoting a shift to partnership and co-creative processes, trying their best to elicit collaboration, while the "troops" are loudly clamoring to remain in their dependent positions, waiting for someone to tell them what to do and resolve all difficulties, thereby hindering organizational progress and making impossible, by definition, true partnership.

Sometimes both employees and managers surrender their power and abdicate their responsibility to change things because being involved in directing changes requires a crucial level of commitment that they feel unwilling or unable to make. Someone has to take the first courageous step. Allan Johnson, in *Privilege, Power, and Difference*, declares that managers and vice presidents "have the power to shape organizational culture and set examples to bring others along" (73). This is a critical element in the shift to partnership, and Cockburn takes the responsibilities of top management even further. She contends that they alone have the initial "power to change organization structures, to set operating rules that influence behavior and build constituencies for further change." Furthermore, she insists that in the move toward shared organizational responsibility and accountability, it is critical that they "make certain kinds of behavior simply unacceptable" (232-33).

Nevertheless, while those managers and vice presidents may have a disproportionate effect as catalysts for initiating change in an organization, at the end of the day *everyone* shares in the responsibility to change the culture, and everyone must takes that responsibility seriously. Johnson admonishes, "If we deny our power to affect people, then we don't have to worry about taking responsibility for how we use it or, more significantly, how we don't" (148). From that view, by refusing to accept responsibility for change, or sometimes even refusing to question behaviors and choices, some people leave an "out" for themselves, such that if things go wrong, they can conveniently blame someone else.

As an organizational consultant, I have heard many comments over the years about how "things would be fine if we could just get some good leadership around here!" When faced with a difficult dilemma, those who consider themselves powerless often try to recruit a better patriarch rather than trying to effect solutions themselves. As Cristina Baldwin describes in *Calling the Circle*, "We spend a great deal of time in this culture trying to abdicate responsibility to the right leader or trying to replace our own changeable thoughts with the perfect wisdom." But heaven help the leader who falls short of expectations, for as Baldwin observes, "We raise up, venerate, and then turn our collective fury at being let down on one fallible human being, or one imperfect experience, after another" (75). Pedestals, blaming, and scapegoating are out of place within a partnership organization. Rather than top-down domination and control, or *power-over*, organizational members in partnership are operating in a system of *power-with* where everyone is called to be in service and in stewardship.

According to the current prevailing images of top executives, leaders who are both in service to the organization and in stewardship of its resources—including both human and natural resources—have been rare, especially in corporate or bureaucratic settings. Nevertheless, while working with the United States Navy Chaplains Corps in the spring of 2003, I observed a number of leaders who were operating in service, both to the organization and to the individuals in "the service." Even though they were firmly lodged in a major patriarchal bureaucracy, with careful attention paid to rank, exemplary individuals within the Chaplains Corps had found a way to provide collaborative leadership from a place of heart and soul. Leadership theorist Sally Helgeson, in *The Female Advantage: Women's Ways of Leadership*, confirms that in her experience, "Our services are ahead of many business organizations in terms of changing the most profound essentials of how they are structured and run" (xix). Indeed, there is a growing awareness in many organizations of the need for individuals who will honor and work from the "soul of leadership," that place where leadership is about *everyone* "taking responsibility to make a difference" (Schindler and King).

Since all members of an organization ultimately contribute to the climate and can potentially provide leadership from any position, attending to leadership concepts and styles is a critical component in successfully achieving the shift to a partnership organization. Quite often an individual who is in a recognized *position* of leadership can, in addition to initiating changes in the structure and culture, provide the first opening for others to acknowledge and reclaim their personal power, thereby encouraging them to exercise leadership as well. For example, business consultant James Autry and translator Stephen Mitchell, in "Beyond Machiavelli: The Source of Real Power," present an approach to leadership that values individuals' gifts. They explain that in accordance with the lessons of an ancient Chinese treatise called the *Tao Te Ching*, "The good leader recognizes that employees already possess innate power: the power of their skills, their commitment to the job, and their passion for the work" (86). When a leader acts based on the recognition of individuals' innate gifts and power, upholding the goal of *power-with*, he or she finds that it is important to get to know individuals as people, rather than just parts that can be replaced, and to know, support, and call out their abilities for the benefit of the whole.

This dynamic is similar to the improvisational movements exhibited in a skilled jazz band. My daughter, who plays jazz bass, tells me that in order to fully experience the potential of jazz, it is important to achieve three things: "you have to really know your instrument, really know the music, and then really listen to each other, so you can know when to take the lead and when to play backup." Similarly, those who would express leadership within organizations need to be well acquainted with the people—the instruments—who bring their talents and unique perspectives to the table, and treat them with respect. They need to be very clear on the mission, or purpose, the values, and the goals of the organization—the music. Finally, they need to listen carefully to the ideas, concerns, and suggested improvisations that arise from the group, and then continue to listen carefully, while operating in such a way that demonstrates the fluidity of leadership, and invites full involvement from everyone. Within such an environment, the responsibility and potential of interwoven *power-with* dynamics and *partnering leadership* is a source of great promise, offering an opening into liberating sources of organizational power that had previously been stifled by competition and control.

Leadership Power and Organizational Forms

This is equal opportunity leadership power; neither position nor physical characteristics determine it. As discussed earlier, there is an urgent need for fundamental changes in the way humans interact with each other and the earth, and recognition that no particular group of human beings is the sole proprietor of "the answers." In that respect, within the long-established system of competition and control, there are sets of leadership and team behaviors that have often been labeled "feminine" or "masculine," and the "masculine" behaviors have been traditionally regarded as the more desirable. The so-called "masculine" behaviors include action-oriented competition, individualism, rational pragmatism, intellectual prowess, and no-nonsense project completion. In contrast, the so-called "feminine" behaviors include empathy, listening, compassion, partnership, social cohesion and connectedness, inclusiveness, collaboration, and valuing relationships over competition.

While some remain convinced that the social strength of these "masculine" attributes has been the source of American successes, others caution that the often one-sided display of those behaviors has resulted in serious losses. Psychologist Robert Johnson in *Femininity Lost and Regained* contends, "Our Western heroic achievements are the envy of the rest of the world, but they were won at the cost of our capacity for warmth, feeling, contentment, and serenity" (6). Although some dismiss the seriousness of losing those capacities, I believe there is a need to rebalance these characteristics in the American cultural psyche, for they do in fact affect employee morale. Far from being a wimpy touchy-feely issue, morale in turn influences key factors such as employee turnover and retention, which in addition to cost considerations are related to organizational efficiency, productivity, and profits.

In spite of common gendered assignments of behaviors as either "masculine" or "feminine," *both* men and women have the capacities to use and exhibit *all* of these behaviors. As professor of women's studies and religion Cynthia Eller insists in *The Myth of Matriarchal Prehistory*, those behaviors "have nothing to do with the potentialities of either gender or with physical sex" (60). Furthermore, neither set of behaviors provides the exclusive solution for all situations; there are circumstances when each of the above behaviors is exactly appropriate for particular conditions. Fortunately, as many leaders are discovering when they exhibit and cultivate an integrated combination of these behaviors, both within themselves and among their co-workers, they have a wider available array of the skills, strength, and abilities needed for particular conditions and positions, which ultimately benefits the organization.

The recognition of this need for a blend of behaviors is one of the markers that indicate a readiness for moving into a partnership paradigm. In many organizations there is a major shift toward valuing both "soft" (feminine), and "hard/technical" (masculine) skills. As an organizational consultant who designed and taught supervisory courses for over 20 years, Melissa Cook observes that in her courses, "*both* elements have been stressed, and over the years I have seen significant shifts in how this blend is accepted and valued" (personal correspondence).

Gender is only one category that has been used to divide employees in traditional organizations. The basic perspectives regarding employees at different levels within an organization are vastly different between traditional hierarchical and partnership organizations, which in turn reflect the assumptions about what is required to manage or lead them. According to organizational development consultant Merrelyn Emery, developer of the "Participative Design" model outlined in *Participative Design for Participative Democracy*, the two basic organizational types are labeled "Design Principle 1" (DP1) and "Design Principle 2" (DP2). They are closely aligned with forms of the patriarchal, or *power-over* organization (DP1) and the partnership, or *power-with* organization (DP2). (Fig. 1)

Design Principle 1 (DP1)	**Design Principle 2 (DP2)**
Closed structure	Open structure
Hierarchical/dominant	Flat/non-dominant
Bureaucratic/representative	Participative/partnership
Rigid/difficult to change	Flexible/adaptable
Top-down decisions made by a few at the top	Consultative/group decisions Self-managing/continuous
Controlling/limited learning	learning

Fig. 1. Organizational Models: DP1 and DP2

According to Emery, similar to Douglas McGregor's "Theory X" organization, policies and attitudes that reflect a specific set of assumptions about employees characterize the DP1 organization. Within that framework, employees are considered to be generally unreliable, irresponsible, dumb, and basically lazy, with the need for some type of competition and motivational reward system to increase their productivity. Based on these assumed characteristics, a strong management presence is required, in order to be sure the work gets done, and the bottom line equals the lowest cost and maximum profits to investors. Managers use rewards and sanctions in an attempt to mold the behavior of employees, who often form informal "shadow groups" to meet their needs for control, belonging, and self-worth. A few people at the top of the hierarchy make top-down decisions, and the responsibility for control and coordination rests at the levels above where the work is actually being done. Emery contends that the results of this kind of scenario primarily include low commitment, involvement, productivity, and quality, with "deskilled" people, who are limited to specific areas of the operation and thus feel divested from the overall outcome.

The DP2 organization employs distinctly different assumptions and policies about the people who work within it. This model moves beyond McGregor's "Theory Y" model, in that rather than focusing on management, it focuses on the group as a whole. Within this context, individuals are considered to be generally purposeful, responsible, and conscious learners, and effective leadership involves coordinating efforts between individuals and teams, promoting active participation and continuous learning, and providing a role model for open communication, innovative problem-solving, and transformative conflict management. DP2 leaders facilitate group decision-making, yet are capable of calling the decision themselves when necessary, in order to prevent the group becoming caught in a quandary that prevents movement. Rather than micromanagement of details, they leave the coordination and control of work processes at the level where the work is actually done. The DP2 leaders help team members to build mutual respect, trust, and support, and to set their team's production goals. According to Emery's research, this type of organization enjoys high levels of commitment, involvement, productivity, and quality, and develops multi-skilled people who are capable of working in many areas of the organization, and who are vested more personally in the overall outcome.

The requirements for leaders in a DP2 or partnership organization distinctly differ from those required of managers in a DP1 or traditional *power-over* organization. Consequently, DP1 managers facing transition into a DP2 organization may perceive such a transformation as a threat to their ability to function within familiar boundaries of a job which they have figured out and been rewarded for doing for a long time. They may have even developed a sense of entitlement, believing that something is owed to them, based on perceived sacrifices they have made. Entitlement and privilege are difficult things to give up.

Shifting into partnership mode requires hard work for everyone involved. As Skip, an employee in the NEFA agency reviewed in chapter 5 observes, "There is some efficiency in benevolent dictatorships." French also admits, "Coercion *seems* a simpler, less time-consuming method of creating order than any other" (509 – italics added), yet it is in the end less effective. Just as the former Soviet Union spent countless hours and untold millions building the Berlin Wall in order to control the citizenry, tyranny in the workplace requires tedious, time-intensive, and costly efforts in order to set up controls to limit, monitor, and obstruct employees; and in the end, employees in such a place want out, not in; they seek ways to circumvent the wall, to escape such a workplace, and to find a freer place to exercise their craft. The Soviet Union built the Berlin Wall in part to stop the talent drain as East Berliners left for West Berlin, and the costly solution worked for a while. Likewise, coercive organizations create similar controls that in the end often foster the very rebellion they were designed to inhibit. To this end, building and sustaining the partnership organization takes time and may in our impatience for immediate results seem inefficient, yet the long-term results pay bigger dividends across every metric corporate stakeholders hold valid.

The shift to partnership represents for employees an answer to a deep yearning for work that is meaningful, that builds connections, and that offers opportunities to experience synergy with a group of actively engaged team-mates. Like Ethan in the NEFA Agency, they often feel a deep sense of relief and are "energized" by the potential of enhancing their efforts, rather than spending time competing and wading through mind-numbing and spirit-sapping bureaucratic details. French observes that "personal encounter, persuasion, listening, and participating in bringing a group to harmony" provide more positive long-term effects, where workers can experience *synergy*, which is "one of the greatest pleasures available to humans" (509).

These are not new ideas. One would think the benefits of leading into partnership would market themselves. Yet French laments that even when faced with evidence to the contrary, individuals in leadership positions all too often "continue to believe . . . that it [power] is substantial, that if we possessed enough of it we could be happy, that if some 'great man' possessed enough of it, he could make the world come right" (509). Caught in that mythology, it should come as no surprise that many believe that it takes a strong, courageous, virtuous, and lone heroic leader to break the spell, to correctly author the future, and to make all things "right." The time has come to co-author a new leadership storyline.

Servant Leaders and Stewardship

Once the principles of partnership are truly integrated into the work aspect of our lives, the shift to partnership ripples through all other levels of our lives. The reconnection to the inner level of our being makes possible our capacity to work together in ways dramatically different from the oppressive *power-over* way we have for too long wrongly assumed was the only way. It requires moving beyond the stereotypical images of "manly men"—or women who adopt the persona of the mythic heroes—who will save us from market meltdowns or terrorist threats, and into a place where individual and collective responsibility for both short- and long-term consequences is seriously accepted throughout the organization. It means recognizing the deep interdependence of all human beings among each other and with the natural world, and then acting accordingly. *Partnering leadership* also means, for example, shrinking the gap between executive compensations and front-line workers' benefits, so that no one is uninsured or underemployed, and executives exhibit generosity, like Ebenezer Scrooge *after* his nocturnal "wake-up call."

Fortunately, in the leadership arena there has been a growing awareness of leadership models that reflect this spirit. One of the first writers to describe this more soulful understanding of leadership was Robert K. Greenleaf, who in 1970 coined the phrase "servant leadership." In his now classic volume *Servant as Leader*, Greenleaf describes servant leadership as the choice "to serve first." He contends that based on selecting service as the primary value, "then conscious choice brings one to aspire to lead." Greenleaf notes that this is "sharply different from the person who is leader first, perhaps because of the need to assuage an unusual power drive or to acquire material possessions."

Greenleaf is clear that the servant leader may or may not hold formal leadership positions, yet the person has found a way to "encourage collaboration, trust, foresight, listening, and the ethical use of power and empowerment." Then, much like those in the NEFA Agency who experience Sophia's visionary and tutelary leadership, "those served grow as persons," and are able to "become healthier, wiser, freer, more autonomous." Ultimately, they are more likely to also exhibit leadership. Greenleaf's "servant leadership" is similar to the "empowering leadership" Starhawk describes, which "means sharing and expanding skills, passing them on as widely as possible, and making space for others to bring in their own creativity, to take material and make it their own, to do things you wouldn't have thought of." Empowering leaders also support risk-taking, and make room for individuals "to make their own mistakes but also their own discoveries" (*Webs of Power* 178).

Taken together, these images of leadership offer a refreshing departure from the traditional autocrat who holds that "leaders" are the ones "in control" and to be obeyed, that he or she alone articulates the vision to be followed and the values that underlie organizational initiatives, that he or she has the right to stake claim to the brilliant ideas of those who work for him or her, and that he or she is entitled to the lion's share of the profits. Families, communities, and organizations have no more need for autocrats, benevolent or otherwise. Indeed, the planet has no more space for *power-over* patriarchal rulers who abuse and exploit people as grossly as they do the natural resources upon which all humans depend for sustaining life on earth.

The image of leader as servant incorporates the notion that anyone can provide leadership, whether taking the reins of an organization, individually speaking up against injustice, or identifying discrepancies in organizational practices and proposing solutions. Servant leadership is antithetical to the attitude displayed in the Nuremburg trials, when the "dominant reply of those accused was 'I was only following orders'" (R. Johnson, *He* 41). Some individuals who have only known highly competitive workplaces might shudder at the concept of service, believing incorrectly that it means surrendering their individuality and abandoning their dreams for advancement. Yet this is not a free-for-all opportunity for everyone to get what they want or to have a turn at being "in charge;" it is based on a deeper commitment to be in service to a greater good or higher calling.

While servant leadership operates from an entirely different premise than the traditional norm, it does not mean the loss of individual spirit, but rather the awakening of it. This kind of service has nothing to do with being in *servitude* to another, to an organization, or even to an ideal. Nor is it related to the "service economy," or even "public service," which in recent stories reported—and often misconstrued—by the press is all too often related to self-interest. Servant leadership means offering oneself freely, including one's skills, energies, and time, in order that the common good might benefit and a higher purpose be achieved. It is, as Wheatley put it, moving "from the leader as hero to the leader as host" (2). Within this context, *public service* refers to a dedication to improving the conditions of common systems, whether human, environmental, or economic, and it becomes a gift, freely given from one's passion and sense of responsibility to something larger than a boss or even an organization. Contrary to the pejorative view commonly held of "government workers," the people of the NEFA agency daily demonstrate true public *service* to each other, to their constituents, and to the earth.

The concept of servant leadership bridges the space between traditional leadership images and the concept of stewardship, which raises the leadership bar another notch. Peter Block, in *Stewardship: Choosing Service over Self-Interest*, explains, "Stewardship is holding something in trust for another." That holding in trust is done while also being willing to "be accountable for the well-being of the larger organization by operating in service, rather than in control, of those around us." Control lies at the crux of this shift, as Block continues, "Stated simply, [stewardship] is accountability without control or compliance" (xx). Rather than operating primarily from self-interest that abdicates responsibility to the larger whole, he urges, "Stewardship asks us to be deeply accountable for the outcomes of an institution, without acting to define purpose for others, control others, or take care of others" (18). This sense of accountability is very different from the *power-over* version of legislated accountability, which depends on authority and compliance. Granted, in a highly competitive society that places a premium on materialistic accumulation and self-aggrandizement, Block's approach to leadership can be met with incredulity and suspicion. Those accustomed to tight controls fear that if regulations are loosened there will be anarchy and unmitigated greed. As one of her peers warned Sophia (of the NEFA Agency), "You'll have everybody wanting everything!"

As Sophia acknowledges, the stewardship path of leadership can be lonely. It represents taking "the road less traveled," when the way ahead is not clear, nor the outcomes guaranteed. Indeed, that road not only feels lonely and rocky, but also seems unmarked and downright confusing for those who have not experienced this kind of leadership. For this journey, leadership consultant Alain Gauthier outlines the shifts required in one's behavior, role, and self-attitude to operate from a base of stewardship. This difficult "high road" trip, Gauthier believes, requires moving "from a driver of change to a 'gardener of people' who sees the potential in others and helps create the conditions for them to grow and reveal themselves." This involves operating as a mentor who assists in birthing others' visions while acting as a "custodian of the shared vision" and assisting in the discernment of emerging patterns and trends. The leader who helps to hold the high watch doesn't bother with pretending to be learned; he or she is an active participant in creating a learning organization that thrives on open discovery and innovation, and "doesn't hesitate to admit 'I don't know'" (398-9).

Moving into this paradigm of leadership is not something one can do by simply choosing it or changing a job title. As with all changes in habit and ritual, this shift requires a personal commitment to, and investment in, supporting transformation. It also represents a deep inner journey: one that taps into the very soul of a profound metamorphosis. And it requires a commitment to continual learning and a lot of practice. A truly soulful leader has grown into their wisdom, while retaining their sense of curiosity and the will for intrepid exploration of new territory. This often means, in Robert Frost's terms, taking the often-unmarked road "less traveled."

Invoking the Soul of Leadership

The notion that there is an expanded, deeper meaning to "leadership" entails recognition that there is also another, deeper level of personal involvement that is different than the one we usually encounter. This is threatening for some. In a society that has traditionally attempted to keep any semblance of emotional or spiritual input outside of the organizational milieu, Block comments, "We have enormous ambivalence about our own choices," particularly when those choices involve the balance between "our beliefs or our ambition." Block wryly concludes, "We want to go to heaven, but we don't want to die" (39). In other words, we want to reap the benefits of partnership without having to surrender our own aspirations, and in a dualistic framework, many people feel caught in the dilemma of having to choose one or the other.

There is also some confusion when the word *soul* is used. It lies between the concepts of *religion* and *spirituality*. *Religion* is a term that for many correlates to organized institutions laden with dogmatic certainties and boundaries. *Spirituality* is often used to refer to the personal experience of one's connection and deep inner knowing or sense of a divine source that is not limited to one ideology or definition, and which has nothing to do with church or religiosity. In the space between those poles, there is an emerging awareness of a possible deeper connection to the workplace, wherein work offers the individual the chance to tap into their unique passions and abilities, and to bring all of who they are to the manifestation of something greater than their specific contribution. There is a danger that this concept and the word itself will be co-opted, as has happened with *diversity*, *team*, and other words and phrases that have become corporate buzzwords. This possibility is demonstrated by Dell computer's online article about itself entitled "The Soul of Dell," in which *soul* is substituted for what most would label organizational culture.

Nevertheless, there is also a growing realization that in order to make the kinds of changes required to realize a true partnership organization, it will be necessary to integrate intellectual perspectives with soulful wisdom and insights. Block believes that, far from outward exhibitions of dogma and attempts to proselytize co-workers to one's preferred brand of religion, "bringing our own spirituality into the workplace is an inward journey," through which "the revolution begins in our own hearts." In this way, the fragmentation between outer and inner personae is overcome, and the soulful journey becomes "the conversation about the integrity of our own actions that ultimately gives us hope" (39). Similarly Wheatley suggests, "People have deep yearnings, a quest for meaning, and an ability to wonder" ("Promise and Paradox" 2). The shift to partnership and to exploring the very *Soul of Leadership*, therefore, begins with deeply personal introspection and choice. Soulful leadership is thus born from the inside out.

Beginning in 1995, and continuing over the past 10 years, I have worked with my colleague Craig Schindler to weave these concepts of leadership into various workshops and presentations titled *The Soul of Leadership*. The main focus for these sessions has been to help people expand their personal leadership capacity and take responsibility for their lives in order to change aspects of their lives that were not working (e.g., facing experiences of discrimination, abusive relationships, workplace conflicts, and a sense of feeling trapped in a system that sucks them dry). We discovered through dialogues with the many participants in these workshops that when individuals at any level in an organization adopt the principles and actions of the *Soul of Leadership*, they are contributing to the co-creation of a partnership organization, for both soulful leadership and partnership take root in the soil of mutual trust and respect. Those conditions feed collaboration and support co-creative innovations and partnering relationships. Regardless of one's position in an organization, we can all practice "servant," "soulful," and *partnering leadership* by following these guidelines:

• Act as agents of conflict transformation, by being the one who takes the initiative to break disruptive, competitive, and destructive cycles, rather than waiting for someone else to go first. Cultivate a frame of reference that holds mistakes and conflicts as learning opportunities.

• Exercise courage by walking through the fear in difficult situations and choosing to move forward with deep integrity in spite of one's apprehension.

• Consciously seek to reduce our own negativity and habitual patterns that might contribute to the organizational "rumor mill." Practice open and conscious self-monitoring.

• Practice open and appreciative inquiry in order to learn from many points of view, open the dialogue, listen with empathy, and speak our truth. Cultivate "beginner's mind," wherein the goal is understanding.

• Generate trust by listening to each other's stories without judgment, blame, or demand. Then tell our own stories, without seeking competition or self-aggrandizement.

In these ways, the "Soul of Leadership" reclaims our hope for the future as we become actively involved in co-creating partnerships. There is no abdicating responsibility to someone "in charge" who can then be crucified if we dislike the outcomes; we are the ones "in charge."

> *The world is like a spiritual democracy.*
> *We vote with our lives.*
> ⚘ Dalai Lama

Leader as Mentor: The Maieutic Model

Another important facet of *partnering leadership* is the conscious and intentional provision of mentoring for those who are new to the organization. The common image of a mentor is someone who takes a younger or relatively inexperienced person "under his or her wing" in order to help the protégé learn the ropes of a new job or how to function in the "real world." There are many models of mentoring, ranging from the Big Brother/Big Sister program that pairs young people with adults who help to guide them through the trials of their teenage years to formalized mentorship programs within corporations as part of their "talent management strategy." Unfortunately, as with anything created with a positive intent, mentoring has at times been corrupted and exploited. For instance, powerful high-ranking executives may welcome as protégés those "golden haired boys" they perceive to be like themselves, and reject including subordinates they perceive as too different from themselves, making clear to the rank and file who is suitable for promotion, and who will need to find their own way (advisably out of that organization).

The word *mentor* comes from the Greek word *men*— to think, remember, counsel—and the Indo-European word *mens*, for "mind." According to depth psychologist Maureen Moss, "the first recorded use of the word mentor appears in Homer's epic, *The Odyssey*" (8). As Odysseus is preparing to leave for the Trojan War, he realizes that he will be gone for a long time and might not return. In consideration of his young son Telemachus, and of his wife Penelope, who is to be left tending the household and their son in a treacherous world, Odysseus sends for his wise friend Mentor to come and guide his son during his father's absence.

Mentor's presence proves to be critical for young Telemachus during the twenty years of Odysseus' journey. Mythologist and cinematographer Phil Cousineau explains, "[Mentor] is the personification of loyalty and the wisest of counsels, but he is also more than a teacher as the story unfolds. His true role is as soul-guide through the underworld for the young prince" (119). During times of severe trials and important growth in the absence of Odysseus, Mentor provides both moral guidance and psychic protection for both Telemachus and Penelope.

Mentor does not act alone; he has a divine double. Athena, "the guiding force of the entire epic," appears "in the likeness of Mentor" (Cousineau 120). Athena is an interesting choice as the archetypal mentor. Moss speculates that perhaps she was chosen "because mentoring is a relationship activity, and relationship is the realm of the feminine." Furthermore she notes that, Athena is widely considered "the Goddess of Wisdom, and the transmission of wisdom is one of the primary tasks of the mentor" (11).

The circumstances of Athena's miraculous birth are also instructive. She was born, full-grown and armored, from her father Zeus's head. Zeus had swallowed her pregnant mother Metis, whose name means "wise counsel," in order to prevent the birth of a child who would usurp his power. In doing so, he appropriated Metis's wisdom. Athena never knew her mother, and thought she did not have one. Thus, she is the archetypal father's daughter, who sees the patriarch as her main benefactor, and therefore owes her primary allegiance to the system he (or she) represents, and tends to downplay her feminine characteristics. Athena mainly appears to Telemachus in the guise of the male Mentor. In that way, she assumes the clothing and persona of the dominant group, much as early female entrants to the workplace were required to do (and still do, in some contexts). Athena, in partnership with Mentor, also signifies the relational aspects of feminine wisdom that can find a way to operate within a traditional organization.

Athena is also recognized as the Goddess of War and the champion of heroes. In this instance, she stands in while the hero-father, on his way home from battle, sojourns with Circe and Calypso. She assists the son in making his initiatory journey from childhood to adulthood as he goes to visit Nestor and Menelaus, hoping to discover the truth about his missing father. Telemachus needs every ounce of courage and strength that he can muster with Athena/Mentor's backing to move from being the daydreaming boy to becoming the thoughtful, energetic young man ready to join his father in vanquishing the suitors who had plagued his mother during Odysseus' absence. Cousineau concludes, "The mythic ventriloquism reveals a mentor's true function," in that just as Telemachus needed "the outer strength of the male consort and the inner wisdom of the goddess" (120), so too initiates in the organizational milieu can grow and flourish with the inspiration and insightful guidance of a wise mentor.

Just as there is a deeper, more soulful level of leadership, so too one finds a more soulful level of mentoring. James Hillman asserts that the job of the mentor is different from that of a parent. "It is enough for a parent to keep a roof over your head and food on the table, and to get you up and off to school. Providing a cave for security, a place for regressions is no small job" (*The Soul's Code* 163). A mentor, on the other hand, is one who perceives one's potential and encourages the steps they see ahead, so that individuals can live out their own "soul's code" and actualize its promise. In other words, the mentor is someone who, as Albert Einstein notes, "acknowledges who we are and what we can be, and ignites the circuits of out highest potential."

In that light, the concept of "maieutic mentoring" is helpful. This is mentoring from a deeply spiritual connection that gently facilitates learning, rather than imposing one's perception of "the way." The maieutic model is generally related to Socrates, and his facilitative approach to learning. It comes from the Greek *maieûtikos*, which means "midwifing," or helping something to be born—without force or having to take credit for it. Philosopher David Fortunoff reasons that just as a midwife "conducts a leading of the body to deliver a new life . . . so is the maieutic method a leading of the mind to discover a new idea" (1). Since Socrates' mother was a literal midwife, Fortunoff observes, "Socrates and his mother comprise both the literal and the figurative senses of *maieûtikos*" and model a "method that produced a changed perspective" (1).

This method contrasts didactic teaching, or what Freire calls "banking" education. It requires a careful attunement to both the context and the individual who is laboring to give birth to a new self, a new idea, or an innovative process or technology. It also requires the maieutic mentor to be in a receptive, supportive mode rather than a directive, credit-taking one. Rabbi Zalman Schachter-Shalomi and journalist Ronald Miller affirm that mentoring "evokes our questing spirit, not by giving answers, but by deepening our ability to question and to search for meaning" (189). Just as the midwife plays no part in conception but facilitates the "outcome," so too the maieutic mentor supports the individual in taking full credit for his or her own accomplishments.

Often, in the absence of the stereotypical willing, experienced mentor we can "look up to," we have to mentor each other and ourselves. We must seek out others who have some insights and experience with the questions we are facing. They may not necessarily be "experts," but are those who can offer wider perspectives than our own, or who can help us with Rilke's admonition to "live the questions." In that light, Schachter-Shalomi and Miller emphasize, "A mentor is not some exalted, superhuman being who magically dispenses wisdom to specially qualified apprentices" (195). Sometimes they are older relatives, friends, colleagues, consultants, or coaches who are able and willing to take on the role of guide. Indeed, the current explosion in the popularity of the coaching profession may be taken as a demonstration at a grass-roots level of the interest in and need for opportunities to both give and receive guidance in this maieutic kind of relationship.

Jean Houston reflects that she considers her work "a kind of midwifery." She explains, "Organizations and cultures, as well as individuals, sometimes need a steadying hand as they birth themselves into a world as strange and unexpected as the one babies face when they emerge from the womb" (*Jump Time* 22). At the personal level, a friend recently queried, "Since we have so few true elders in our culture, who will be the elders for us, as we make our transitions?" I responded, "We will be the elders and mentors for each other—and then we will turn to the next generation, and help them along. We are all in this together." It is important to remember that we each possess an inner wisdom, which awaits our opening and invitation to emerge. In that respect, mentoring is a sacred partnership, within us and with each other. In the wise words of an old Chinese proverb,

Go to the people. Live among them.
Learn from them. Love them.
Start with what they know. Build from what they have.
But of the best leaders, when the task is accomplished
and their work is done, the people remark,
"We have done it ourselves."

❧ Chapter 5 ❧

Organizational Partnerships: The Living Proof

When faced with simultaneous global crises on multiple fronts, the actions of organizations—whether corporations, government entities, educational institutions, or private nonprofit agencies—serve as the front line for making far-reaching, lasting changes in the way the global community "does business." Although individual and family relationships are vitally important in shifting the tenor of collective interactions and expectations, the majority of adults spend large amounts of their time engaged in organizational pursuits, and consequently partnerships in those contexts have especially wide-ranging effects. Therefore, while there are some references to relationships at other levels, from the family to the international level, this book focuses on enhancing our understanding and offering viable and powerful alternatives required to reform authoritarian organizational structures. In addition, we must identify areas where learning (through education initiatives and mentoring) can assist individuals in re-evaluating assumptions and co-creating collective shifts.

There remains a critical need for examples and visions that demonstrate how the *Partnership Model* can work, particularly as organizational leaders attempt to re-calibrate their business plans to face a world demanding more flexibility and quicker response times. In such chaotic times, many business leaders are more willing to consider alternatives, even those that call for a paradigm shift from traditional hierarchical and authoritarian management styles, so long as those alternatives do not threaten personal or organizational progress. Although many steadfastly deny the potential for true partnership organizations to succeed, there are nevertheless exemplary instances where co-creative partnerships are already being successfully implemented in organizations. These examples demonstrate that partnerships are not antithetical to productivity or profit, nor are they dismissive of individual growth.

One of the important things to keep in mind, when considering the move to partnership organizational models, is that unlike dualistic models, this is not an "all or nothing" proposition. In fact, Eisler and Montuori assert, "No organization will orient completely to the partnership or dominator model" (6). Thus, there is a *spectrum* of partnership representations that demonstrate the processes involved in shifting the organizational culture. They range from small changes in the way meetings are run or the degree of *voice* workers have in the implementation of their jobs to fundamental, wholesale system and culture shifts. Opportunities to incorporate partnership principles vary within the constraints of different kinds of organizations; examples of partnership initiatives can be identified in every arena (e.g., capitalist corporations, educational institutions, private nonprofit organizations, and publicly funded agencies). Some consider the constraints of capitalism and the importance of "the bottom line" to be the most restrictive of all, yet Eisler shares five corporate examples in *The Power of Partnership* (66-68), which I have updated here:

• Before its acquisition by Ford Motor Company, teams of Swedish workers at **Volvo** decided their own work schedules, division of labor, and production timetables—with higher productivity and fewer defective products. Now that Ford owns Volvo, its workflow designs reflect more traditional manufacturing and organizational models, and many Volvo loyalists believe reliability has declined. Minimally what seems lost was a genuine effort to leverage workplace partnerships that benefited not only customers and shareholders, but people at work by changing conditions of employment.

• The **Dupont** plant in Towanda, Pennsylvania instituted self-directed teams where employees do their own problem solving and even have input in hiring processes—with 35% higher productivity.

• Dee Hock, former head of **Visa** credit card network and author of *Birth of the Chaordic Age*, explains how many people with different knowledge in banking and finance came together to create Visa (originally BankAmerica Card). Hock shared how competing interests were not defeated, but rather incorporated and in the end established an organization where all owner-members are linked in a "chaordic" structure that allows them to simultaneously both cooperate and compete. Visa is essentially a global network organization. Hock and others applied these same principles when they formed the nonprofit **Chaordic Commons**, which is a network of people interested in learning about and creating sustainable partnership organizations. The Chaordic Commons is comprised of "People around the world pioneering new ways to organize that liberate the human spirit, advance deeply shared purposes, foster the common good, and nourish all life" (www.chaordic.org).

• Bill Brandt, the CEO of **American Woodmark**, incorporated a specific unit on the concepts of "caring" into the corporate management-training program—with the result that job satisfaction and productivity greatly increased.

• Many business owners, aware of the concerns and demands of family care-giving, are offering either childcare subsidies or on-site childcare centers, family leave policies, or other supportive mechanisms that recognize the dilemmas encountered by those who attempt to juggle family and work demands. For example, employees at **Baxter International** are able to take time off to be with their children not only when they are sick, but also for school, sporting, or other events. Although there are significant challenges for the organization, regarding issues of liability and state or federal regulations, many corporations have found assisting employees with their childcare issues to be worthwhile, both for higher morale and increased cost effectiveness, relative to reduced turnover.

Further evidence of shifts in how people are valued and rewarded for working together can be found through service providers like **Hewitt Associates** and **Herman-Miller**. Hewitt Associates is a consulting company specializing in employee compensation and benefits, and helped set the benchmarks used each year by *Fortune* magazine when it reports the "100 Best Places to Work." Herman-Miller is best known for selling and leasing office furnishing, but few are aware that it, like its competitor **Steelcase**, offer turnkey office design solutions that build "team space" into work areas. As a result, architects have built whole corporate campuses with emphasis on balancing individual space, team space, and community space (e.g., cafeterias and cafés). Team space is not simply meeting rooms, but open areas where groups can come together spontaneously or for structured creative efforts to work. These new office designs, found in the U.S. and Western Europe, stand in stark contrast to the impersonal, de-motivating cubicle dwellings that embodied all that was unimaginative and dehumanizing about modern offices. These new designs hint at the promise that partnership organizations can find root when cubicle walls come down.

At the other end of the organizational spectrum, there are many smaller grassroots and community-based organizations that have been consciously founded on partnership principles, both in their operation and their mission. The majority of these organizations are private nonprofit entities, which offer a natural but certainly *not* guaranteed predisposition to the partnership model. Based on a combination of their mission, organizational structure, and norms, I selected four examples from a wide array suggested by participants of the 2003 (first) international "Gather the Women Congress," held in San Francisco (see www.GathertheWomen.org).

• "The Bridge: Jewish and Arab Women" creates opportunities for Israeli and Palestinian women to meet together as women whose hearts have been broken with the losses of their husbands, sons, brothers, and fathers resulting from on-going cycles of hatred and revenge. This grassroots organization fosters dialogues as a means of collectively seeking ways to stop the bloodshed and build partnerships based on creating peace that will counteract the deadly policies destroying their homes and devastating their families. (See www.iflac.com/the-bridge.html).

• The "PeacexPeace" (Peace by Peace) organization (www.peacexpeace.org) is dedicated to "educating, empowering, and connecting women across cultures, ethnicities, geography, religions, and generations," and has published a documentary titled "Women on the Frontlines" that celebrates women as peace builders. This organization grew out of a "founding dialogue" held in January 2002 at the home of Patricia Smith Melton, who now serves as executive director of the organization. Melton makes clear that PeacexPeace is a fundamentally partnership organization —both within the organization and with its external partners —that is dedicated to tapping into "the on-the-ground power of women" in a "global revolutionary movement." That movement holds as its mission the connection between "circles of peace" in all nations.

• The "Pachamama Alliance" (www.pachamama.org) focuses on "preserving the Earth's tropical rainforests by empowering indigenous people, who are its natural custodians." As an alliance of individuals, organizations, and networks committed to conserving and restoring rainforest resources, they declare their partnership with each other, between nations, and with the natural world. Their efforts range from encouraging "conscious consumerism" to support indigenous tribal groups' efforts, rather than imposing externally concocted solutions that meet members' needs but may be largely irrelevant to local interests.

• The "Foundation for Conscious Evolution" (www.evolve.org) is a network developed to connect community members in Santa Barbara, California, interested in answering the question posed by futurist Barbara Marx Hubbard: "What would happen if this community were to become more fully aware of its own potential for conscious evolution?" This organization has consciously woven Dee Hock's chaordic principles and practices into its governing structure. Although it was started under the guidance and inspiration of Barbara Marx Hubbard, FCE has been able to move away from dependence on a single guiding light. A volunteer council provides the foundation's direction and the community network shapes its topical affinity-based core groups. Besides testimonials at both the 2003 and 2004 Gathering the Women Congresses in support of this foundation, I have personal experience with this organization, as a three-year member of a local core group, where I learned first-hand the value of taking time to establish *resonance* in the relationships between group members, along with attending to structures and norms.

In spite of these and many other partnership examples, there are skeptics who deny the possibility that the *Partnership Model* can truly succeed in more "formal" organizations. They consistently point out the inherent difficulty in developing and sustaining alternate organizational patterns, as they (correctly) project the challenges of operating within a new paradigm, without having changed from the beliefs and practices of the old. This is a valid concern, and deserves specific attention. Yet it has not proven to be the definitive end of emergent partnership organizations, whether instituted in relatively small private nonprofit organizations or along the spectrum of partnerships in the larger corporate examples provided above.

Skepticism sharpens our thinking and even supports the unique partnership described so far, but it should not be an excuse for inaction; then it is not skepticism, but the kind of pessimism that sends individuals scurrying for the security of the known world regardless of how false that security may be. The readiness of some to reject the journey to partnership because it seems too difficult, too impossible to fathom— even though their current situation is stifling organizational creativity and flexibility—is akin to a crew stranded on a cold desolate island near Antarctica fully aware that they are unlikely to be found and yet unwilling to set out in small boats on a risky journey to save themselves.

To the skeptics, consider the transformation of a federal agency from deep-rooted bureaucratic entrenchment to partnership. The following case example traces a conscious and momentous shift undertaken by a group of federal employees. Their expanded story is included here because I have personally worked with organizational members as they reorganized and made the transition to a partnership model, and am therefore knowledgeable about the details of their journey.

An Organizational Journey Into Partnership:
A Case Study of NEFA

The Northeastern Federal Agency (NEFA) employs about sixty people who provide technical assistance to citizens and organizations in the Northeastern United States. Their collective shift into a partnership operation began in 1996, and has been successfully sustained to date (writing in early 2005). Along with shifting their organizational model, the numbers of women and people of color employed within their ranks have also increased. There was (in 1996) and still is considerable emphasis on workforce diversity within the entire federal agency. While diversity was not particularly problematic at NEFA in 1996, the percentages have increased considerably in the past 8 years. At this time, their make-up consists of 20% people of color and 51% women. The women are employed at all levels within the agency, and the 20% diversity rate is among the highest levels of any statewide organization within this national federal agency. Their transition has not been without many challenges and pitfalls; yet, those who have participated in this organization report higher morale and productivity—even in the face of a shrinking budget and periodic punitive harassment from the authoritarian, patriarchal agency based in Washington D.C.

Until the autumn of 1995, this statewide agency had operated as a traditional top-down, hierarchical organization. As a relatively unimportant state within the overall agency power structure, the executive position was often used as a stepping-stone for more influential assignments. When that top state position was filled with a new leader who was determined to change the organizational culture, there were skeptics and naysayers. "Those are great ideas, but they can never happen here," she was told. "There is too much history that has led to a lack of trust," and "Washington will never stand for having someone operate outside the box."

Nevertheless, she started by holding a Search Conference, wherein high-level representatives from a variety of key statewide stakeholder groups came together to tell their stories and describe their hopes for a different future. Subsequent to the Conference, the statewide (NEFA) group was able to collect those stories and visions and to catalogue both the resources they are charged with conserving and the inherent skills and talents already existing within their membership. Beginning with identifying both critical needs and potential partnerships with stakeholder groups who share interest in sustaining those resources, they have been able to develop an active and effective partnership network within their state, and with private and nonprofit entities that share their concerns. Agency stakeholders include state and local public agencies; private entrepreneurs; and private, nonprofit groups. All stakeholders are engaged as partners in stewarding shared ecosystems and economic resources.

At this time (early 2005), in spite of being required to operate within a traditionally top-down, authoritarian federal framework, this organization has succeeded—within the state boundaries at least—in making the transition to a largely partnership design wherein all voices are heard, everyone has opportunities to exhibit leadership, and participation is encouraged at all levels of planning and problem-solving. In spite of early difficulties with a few competitive and manipulative individual employees, the transformation has occurred, so that both employees and community partners are valued, included as members of the whole, and treated with respect. Although individuals do still receive recognition for exemplary efforts, recognition is also given within the context of team accomplishments.

From the beginning, NEFA leaders realized that the shift from the traditional organizational structure to a partnership organization was too important, and the transition process fraught with too many perils, to be either left to chance or initiated without adequate support and follow-up. Therefore, a series of training sessions and working group projects was mapped out and implemented. I was honored to help with the design of that effort, and to provide the training and facilitation for all of the following sessions, which took place over a two-year period:

• Everyone in the state attended a three-day **Communication Workshop**, which included topics such as basic communication skills (perception-checking, active listening, and intercultural perspectives), taking personal responsibility and building trust, understanding personal preferences and styles, and skills for managing change, transitions, and conflicts. This workshop was presented three separate times in order to facilitate attendance by all employees, and for the session sizes to be more conducive to participative and in-depth experiential learning.

• Everyone attended a single three-day **Participative Design Workshop**, which was based on the principles and processes outlined in *Participative Design for Participative Democracy*, edited by organizational development consultant Merrelyn Emery. Individual commitment statements were written and read aloud to the group at the end of this session. The products of this workshop provided the impetus for working groups that would meet independently over the ensuing period of several months. The task of those self-facilitating working groups was to take suggestions and input from all employees and collectively design a new organizational structure that would support a partnership operating system. This massive undertaking included completely redesigning working relationships, assessing competency requirements and rewriting job descriptions, starting with changing the name, focus, and intent of the management team. Inspired by Peter Block's concept of "stewardship," as described in chapter 4, the management team chose to be called the "Stewardship Team," with the goal of operating in service, rather than seeking compliance or control.

• To help understand and manage the inevitable transition process, everyone attended a one-day workshop, **Managing Organizational Transitions**, based on the ideas and processes presented by William Bridges in *Managing Transitions: Making the Most of Change*. That workshop included an understanding of what is involved in transition management, an assessment of both individual and organizational transition readiness, an in-depth examination of the stages of transition (which are further described in chapter 7), development of an action plan, and concluded with a ceremonial rite of passage to herald their movement into a new paradigm.

• Once the new team-based partnership organization was designed and everyone had accepted membership in one or more of the newly designated teams, each team had a separate **Teambuilding** session. This session opened with clarifying how a true *team* is different than a *group*. This was based on a definition of *team* that I authored a number of years ago: *"Team* is not equal to a loosely confederated group of individuals, fiercely protecting their turf." Each team developed its own set of roles and responsibilities, team norms, and beginning action plans. All of those results were printed and shared with the other teams, so that everyone had a clear sense of how the work would flow and who would be the *champions* (as opposed to authoritarian project managers) for different projects and initiatives.

• Everyone attended a two-day session, **Conflict Management and Principled Negotiation**, which both reviewed key communication skills and offered expanded understanding about the key differences between misunderstandings, disagreements, and conflicts; the impacts of personal conflict styles; and different modes of managing conflicts, such as win-lose versus win-win problem solving, and the elements of *Principled Negotiation*, based on *Getting to Yes,* by Roger Fisher and William Ury, leaders of the Harvard Negotiation Project.

• Everyone attended a one-day session, **Meeting Management**, which covered elements of organizing effective meetings (such as having previously agreed-upon meeting agreements or ground rules, agenda-setting, and roles for meeting management), various decision-making methods (including consensus building and consultation), how to select the most appropriate decision-making method for any given situation, and the importance of *everyone* practicing *facilitative behavior*, which involves both self-monitoring and shared responsibility for keeping the group on track and following meeting agreements.

• Those who either demonstrated an interest or whose jobs required that they have facilitation skills attended a two-day **Facilitator Training**. This experiential session covered a philosophy of facilitation, a deeper understanding of what constitutes *facilitative behavior* for all meeting participants, and a "cook book" of facilitation techniques for use in various settings.

• A two-day **Community-Building** session was held, which included some members of the NEFA and some members of other stakeholder community groups. Information about the principles and practices of building community using dialogue skills were presented, along with facilitated opportunities to strengthen the sense of partnership between the groups represented. (More information about building partnership communities is presented in chapter 6).

At the end of all of these workshops, and when the teams were up and running in their new configurations, the agency organized an "Endings-Beginnings Day" in the autumn of 1997. This event provided another collective rite of passage, designed both to consciously mark the changes they were making together and to help with managing the transition process.

Eight years after the initial series of communication skills workshops, this agency has been through quite an odyssey of changes, challenges, disappointments, regroupings, and triumphs. To give those who made this journey a voice, and to identify particular difficulties and successes, I conducted sixteen interviews in the autumn of 2003. Some of the interviewees were part of the original group who participated in designing the new structure and made the transition, and others were newcomers, who brought a fresh, relatively "outside" perspective to their experiences within this partnership organization. Excerpts from their observations follow, using pseudonyms, to protect individuals' privacy.

When asked to compare their experiences working within traditional top-down, power-over organizations and this particular partnership organization, employees offered a wide range of experiences and perspectives. Those who have been working for this organization since before the shift offer some long-term observations. Andrea, who has worked in this agency for about ten years, comments, "Under the old patriarchal organization, I only really spoke to my direct supervisor. Now I feel more empowered by the 'top brass.' Sometimes I've felt a little overwhelmed by being so empowered, but it has helped me grow and face the challenges. I have had the freedom to grow where I needed to grow." Steve, one of the younger members of the team who has experienced both "before" and "after" systems recalls, "With the old hierarchical structure, the top people could almost hide behind their positions and the chain of command. With the partnership structure, there is more freedom, access to resources, and accountability." That freedom can admittedly sometimes be messy, time-consuming, and frustrating. Skip, who also survived the transition period, muses that "sometimes there is efficiency with some forms of dictatorship," and he acknowledges, "There is work in forming a partnership because people have different ideas about what should be done."

Indeed, sustaining open dialogue can be confusing, time consuming, and hard work. Working in partnership is not for those who prefer to just be told what to do—or who want to be the ones doing the telling. Antonio, who has worked fifteen years with the agency, observes, "People bring so much baggage of their whole life—with ideas about their separate disciplines and what-not—we almost *have* to retrain them to understand our reality, which is not just based on sheer competition for numbers." All of these comments highlight the inevitable sense of disorientation that accompanies a transition into an entirely new *modus operandi*. Yet with careful attention to relationships, openness about the process, and flexibility in its implementation, widely disseminated information about the necessary skills and new underlying assumptions, and a sense of "we're all in this together," that confusion and discomfort has generally proven to be manageable for most people navigating the transition.

On the other hand, some people welcome the opportunities presented by the release from top-down management. Ethan, a 20-year veteran of the agency, recalls, "I've always been self-motivated, with clear goals. But before, in the patriarchal organization, I ran into walls and barriers. I was a cog in the machine. [In that system], if you're in the wrong place to reach your goals, you're pretty well screwed." At one point, he was so discouraged he was ready to quit—not only from his particular job, but also from the entire agency. His recollection of the transition process is, "I was energized! Since then, I've been able to play out my goals and work in a variety of interdisciplinary teams." Ethan looks to the future and hopes that "someday we will be able to have trans-disciplinary teams, where people actively teach each other."

Nelson, who has worked twenty-seven years with the agency, concurs. He recalls that under the old structure, "there was not a lot of interaction on goal-setting; many people were pretty much told what to do." For some, being told what to do represents release from having to figure out the challenges of the situation and the impacts of various choices. For others, who have unique perspectives and ideas and want to be involved in the planning and decision-making processes, being excluded can be acutely frustrating, in that they are not able to fully participate in improving processes that could change outcomes. Nelson continues, "Now, it is helpful to have wide input that also allows for flexibility when things have to change or shift quickly. People have more understanding and ownership of the goals, so they therefore work more clearly to meet those goals." In summary, those who have fully engaged in the partnership process have found opportunities they never had in the past, have developed many new and satisfying working relationships, and recognize (contrary to common perception) that the partnership organization is much more flexible and better able to adapt quickly to the needs of its stakeholders and constituencies than were the traditional organizational structure and processes.

Short-term perspectives offer some of the most clear-cut comparisons. Amber, who has only worked at this agency for a little over a year, remembers working in other *power-over* organizations, where she was a minority, she felt "removed from the outcome," and "did not feel valued as a person." She recalls, "Turf issues interrupted the ability to make progress," whereas "here, the learning never stops. The work is not routine, and I am able to work with so many different people. I *love* the partnerships because I don't have to have all the expertise in all areas."

Sheila, who also has one year with this agency, describes the difference between her past experiences and working in this environment as "like night and day." She also extended that comparison to her experiences working within *this* state-level agency as opposed to her exposure to other ways of operating that she has encountered at national-level agency training sessions and project meetings. She is very clear that this particular state agency is relatively unique within the national agency framework, both in the day-to-day working environment and in her ability to fully utilize her skills.

While many of the men expressed their frustrations with various aspects of prior *power-over* organizations, the woman interviewed had specific tales of feeling devalued and particularly limited in former work environments. While these stories are widely supported by research documenting discriminatory practices against women, minorities, and those who are differently abled, it is also important to remember that the larger problem represented by these incidents is not just with the individual men who exhibited this behavior, but with the *system* that supported them, and did little to protect the rights of the women who had these experiences. Cheryl, who has worked in the NEFA organization for three years, shudders to remember some of her work in the private sector. She describes a situation where "the boss would literally jump up and down and scream at employees," conceding, "It was clearly not a fair system. I was paid less than all the men, including those who were less skilled than I was." Bernadette, a five-year employee, remembers a previous job where in spite of her skill and training, she was expected to fix her boss's coffee, while he was constantly dictating her clothing and hairstyles. She impishly concedes, "I put salt in his coffee." Cheryl admits, "Sometimes the partnership system is less immediately efficient, because of the juggling required due to multiple time schedules. But we ultimately get a better product, by having input and buy-in up front." She avows she is much happier, and feels much more productive, working for the NEFA.

Meanwhile, Honor, who has also completed three years with this organization, came from a background as a university professor. Her comparisons stem from experiences of being belittled by a domineering department head, where she implicitly knew it was not appropriate to even speak up or add input, let alone object. She described one clear and uncomfortable example of this treatment. At a departmental meeting, where all the faculty present held Ph.D.s— including Honor—the Department Chair introduced them to a visitor as "Dr.---, Dr.---, Dr.---, and Honor." She noted that it was common, even though she had the same credentials and job title as others, to be referred to in ways that inferred she was not truly part of the group.

Coming to work for the NEFA has been an enormous personal and professional opening for Honor. She explains, "When I first came here, people were remarkably helpful. Working together is a completely different model from the competition I experienced before." She explained that not only is everyone welcome to speak up and participate in dialogues and problem-solving; clarifying questions at any level are expected, and "a breadth of input" is requested "when ideas have been asked to be put on the table." Furthermore, "frequently, someone actually goes to the trouble to record all the ideas on an easel pad so none will be lost." Like many other employees of this agency, she has a sense of following her calling and doing work that is deeply satisfying within a highly supportive milieu. The individual transitions for these individuals, as they moved from traditional power-over organizations into the partnership model, have been marked by a sense of relief and personal growth. Although there are many similar stories among NEFA employees, that sense of relief was not always the case for those who underwent the transition from its inception within the agency.

The transition process was neither quick nor easy, as those who helped to lead and manage the process witnessed and experienced. Art, who has also been with the agency for over thirty years, explains, "With the transition, the biggest thing to overcome was understanding *what* was changing. We were *not* getting rid of all structure, but forming a different structure." He firmly believes, "Part of what really helped the transition was that people kept *talking* about what was happening." It is important to note that the level of "talking" required had nothing to do with feeding that common bane of organizational health: the rumor mill. There were on-going, conscious efforts to engage everyone in both formal and informal dialogues to evaluate how things were going and collectively devise new solutions for both old and emerging problems. In that respect, they were both managing their transitions and "growing the *common ground*."

Those internal difficulties in understanding the new format were initially reflected by cautious external stakeholders, who needed some time and a track record to see that things really were changing—that things were not descending into chaos, but actually *working*—and that in fact, the service from the agency became more efficient and accessible that it had been in the past. Nelson points out, "Now our partners know they can count on us not to play games with them and to have clearer expectations, but it has taken a while for people to both understand and trust our different way of operating." This organization has gradually built solid alliances with a variety of stakeholders, even as their relationships with each other evolve.

Meanwhile, the most difficult aspect of the transition has involved the relationships with the agency headquarters personnel and with other states, both of which seem to consider this group an aberration; something to be discounted, suffocated, and ignored, so that other state agencies will not try to do the same thing. Lindsay, an employee who has worked in this agency for thirty years observes, "The transition period lasted about two years. It was rough because some employees were comfortable with the old structure. When they had to take new responsibilities to make decisions, it was very stressful for them." Yet she also declares, "The most difficult part of the transition for me was *not* the operation itself, but making the structure fit what headquarters wanted, because they wanted everything to fit in their little boxes." She has also been party to some of the harassment received from the headquarters in Washington, D.C. She acknowledges, "D.C. says we are 'not efficient,' but they have no idea how much better we are operating."

Sophia, the top executive and an agency employee for twenty-seven years, describes agency managers at headquarters as holding perspectives that were more than uninformed. "They're not really interested in knowing how we've been successful—in improving our efficiency, our effectiveness, our innovative projects, or our vastly improved relationships with our stakeholders—because the agency is still stuck in a mechanized, 'Theory X' mode, working the old ways harder while hoping they'll get better results." Indeed, although the NEFA has turned in consistently exemplary, high performance for the past eight years, the agency at large has been largely unwilling to acknowledge this group's documented achievements in consistently reaching their program goals.

In fact, by viewing this state through a constantly critical lens, there has been very little internal agency acknowledgement of the significant strides this group has made, even though local stakeholder agencies and town councils have given them very favorable evaluations of their effectiveness. Additionally, some of their innovative products have been presented in Washington, D.C., where they received commendatory recognition. Furthermore, Sophia has been recognized with two "Honor Awards," from the cabinet secretary who heads the overall agency, with almost no acknowledgement from agency bureaucrats and functionaries.

With any concerted effort to shift a traditional organizational culture, there are particular challenges for the person designated as the *leader*. In this instance, Sophia has borne the brunt of the external challenges in order to create a relatively safe *container* within which the rest of the state's employees could realize their fullest potential and operate at exceptionally high levels. She has paid a high price, both personally and professionally. She notes, "One of the most painful things I have experienced within the patriarchy is the sense that I do not belong. I'm always on the outside, and it doesn't matter what I've accomplished; I'll never be given credit for what I've done."

Nevertheless, in spite of the frustrations dealt by the agency bureaucrats, she reports she has experienced great job satisfaction, relative to the collective accomplishments of the people in the NEFA and a network of colleagues. She muses, "I do have my supporters sprinkled throughout the country, thank heavens! The chance to really get to know the amazing people I'm working with, to have that shared sense of purpose is *huge*, and it sustains me." Admittedly, choosing not to follow the traditional path can be both lonely and painful, and taking the "road less traveled" requires clear vision, courage, and perseverance. Indeed, this woman is the most authentically powerful leader I have ever met.

In spite of her local successes, appreciation, and respect, the larger agency's lack of inclusion and validation transfers not only into a lack of recognition, but also into reduced personal remuneration. Sophia insists, "Because the agency isn't ready for an innovative, progressive woman leader, my earning power has been greatly diminished, which is reflected in the fact that my GS level [federal salary grade] is lower than most other states' executives." She also constantly faces the skepticism of fellow state executives and those at the upper echelons of the agency hierarchy. She explains, "No one trusts the people. For them, the employees are 'corporate assets' or 'human capital.' They de-humanize people, and then wonder why the agency struggles to maintain decent morale and production. We meet or exceed our goals every year, plus we innovate and succeed at things others can't yet even imagine."

As an example of those statistics, when the Department in Washington, D.C. (the agency headquarters) contracted to conduct an independent, nationwide survey two years after the NEFA was reengineered, the NEFA state unit had the highest number of surveys returned, and was shown to be one of the top three units in the entire Department having the highest morale, job satisfaction, levels of trust, and feelings of empowerment and being personally valued. In addition, employees reported that they felt their ideas were taken seriously and that they were able to weigh in on all decisions. There was a very large gap between the top three units and the rest of the States' units. These survey results are particularly noteworthy because the survey was conducted, as Sophia noted, "at a time shortly after we had pulled the plug on all that was familiar, and during a time period with a major increase in workload from new programs." She proudly remembers, "The climate survey provided a real litmus test on how well we had managed the change and transition. We passed with flying colors! The new structure was working, and both the quality and quantity of production improved dramatically, while the survey showed that employees were happy and well adjusted to the team structure. In fact, they were significantly happier than the rest of the organization as a whole."

Furthermore, Sophia proudly recalls that when they endured a recent audit, based on a fraudulent whistle-blower complaint, "Our process and integrity held up through the investigation, and we were congratulated by the investigators at the end for being one of the most professional groups they had ever seen." Sophia manages to paradoxically balance highly professional competence and what some consider quirky insights, which is confusing to many people. Her supervisor once asked, "How can someone be both so fearless and tough *and* so compassionate and kind at the same time?" Sophia observes, "Holding both aspects is inconceivable to the patriarchs!" Indeed, she is something of an enigma within the rigidly hierarchical federal government: a *truly* compassionate leader who nevertheless produces exemplary results.

Within this context, one of the ongoing concerns is whether operating in partnership can continue to survive the larger social and bureaucratic forces that seem to conspire at times to derail any efforts toward empowering partnerships and to reinstitute the old command-and-control, *power-over* model. Nelson notes, "There seem to be more and more forces that would drive us back to the old structure and the 'wait until told' philosophy. We know (and they know) it doesn't work, but they are still tied to it, and so they are forcing it." The people in the NEFA have been constantly challenged by the larger parent organization, where very few managers have been either able or willing to understand the principles, processes, or promises of the paradigm shift this intrepid group has undertaken. Nevertheless, they have developed a remarkable performance track record and set of working relationships, both within their membership and between their agency and other public and private entities, which have resulted in new alliances, stronger working relationships, and a notable respect among local community leaders.

In spite of the challenges they have faced—and a few holdout employees—the large majority of this group has supported each other, pulled together, and persevered in providing high quality service to the citizens and stewardship of the resources in their state. In many respects the constant threat from the agency superstructure has only strengthened their resolve. The lessons they have learned and the skills they have attained will survive. Sandy, who has a somewhat unique perspective by virtue of the fact that she had worked for Sophia once before in another state, reports, "It was great. Even when she left that state and things went back [to the old structure and norms], we had all learned that things *could* be different, so it never went totally back to the way it was before." This is the promise for the future: here is a group of people who have experienced the dignity, respect, and stimulating growth potentials within a partnership system. No matter what happens, they will never go totally back to who they were before; they will always know there is another way. The French philosopher poet René Daumal describes this phenomenon:

> *You cannot stay on the summit forever;*
> *you have to come down again.*
> *So why bother in the first place?*
> *One climbs and one sees. One descends,*
> *one sees no longer, but one has seen.*
> *There is an art of conducting oneself*
> *in the lower regions by the memory*
> *of what one saw higher up.*
> *When one can no longer see,*
> *one can at least still know.*

150

In a world of increasing stress and chaos,
there is a profound and growing need for real community.

Personal leadership requires us
to take the initiative to reach out and create
a sense of authentic connection with a few people
in our lives.

Community provides a space of refuge
for renewing our vision.

Hope is what we live:
community empowers us to do it.

&. Craig Schindler and Cynthia King
Hope Out of the Ashes: Being a Light in the Darkness

◈ Chapter 6 ◈

Building the Partnership Community

Like the words *partnership*, *power*, and *leadership*, *community* is one of those terms about which everyone holds some idea or image. According to Webster's Dictionary, a *community* is "a body of persons having common rights, benefits, and privileges." Upon closer examination, it is apparent that for many people *community* represents some loosely affiliated group: the Black community, the gay community, or even my neighborhood, where many people are acquainted, but few really know each other well. Within that frame of reference, the idea of "building community" is something of an enigma; how do you build something that already exists by virtue of a prescribed set of common characteristics? Does "building community" represent another variation on the exclusive, gated-community theme? Furthermore, what does community have to do with creating partnerships?

This is an important concept to clarify because the objective in promoting partnerships is not to create a new brand of exclusivity, such as cults or groups that coalesce around "alternative" values to those held by the larger society. During the decade of the 1970s, for example, there was a flurry of activity loosely focused around the communal movement. While the majority of those groups have disbanded, some *intentional communities* founded around specific ideologies during that time are still thriving. Nevertheless, as sociologist Marilyn French observes, "Organic communities were not part of the dominant vision of the West, which defines community as a set of interactions by antagonistic or occasionally complementary interest groups—as a mere by-product of the 'rational' search for gain" (544). Furthermore, she points out that "most experimental communities have worked on a principle of *exclusion*," which is in itself "a patriarchal value" (544 – italics added). That observation of exclusivity resulted in French's dismissive conclusion that "no [community] movement has ever been more than an accumulation of small motions of people acting within their own spheres" (545). The answer to that dismissal lies in an expanded definition of *community*.

The *Partnership Model* described herein is much larger than advocating the creation of small, self-focused communities. It represents a fundamental culture shift, and it is prompted by a growing commitment to support the survival and *thrival* of the human race, in every region, and ultimately in every nation around the globe. There are currently multiple efforts to enter into and intentionally build *community*. In these contemporary arenas, *community* indicates a way of being together, which is something much deeper than just happening to reside next to each other or share a set of common characteristics. It is a sense of having a deeply shared feeling of belonging and of knowing there is a safe place where one can go and feel known, feel "at home," and find acceptance—even when there is internal disagreement—which is a key factor in differentiating this notion of community from exclusive groups or rigidly managed cults.

The Foundation for Community Encouragement, an organization that grew from M. Scott Peck's teachings in *The Road Less Traveled*, describes this perspective of community, and the need for it, in their "Founding Dream:"

> There is a yearning in the heart for peace. Because of the wounds—the rejections —we have received in past relationships, we are frightened by the risks. In our fear, we discount the dream of authentic community as merely visionary. But there are rules

by which people can come back together, by which the old wounds are healed. It is the mission of The Foundation for Community Encouragement to teach these rules—to make hope real again—to make the vision actually manifest in a world which has almost forgotten the glory of what it means to be human. (www.fce-community.org)

In my experience of their community-building processes, I observed that the occurrence of bringing a group of relative strangers into a deep sense of *community* within a fairly short period of time could consistently be replicated. In that context, *community* does not require any particular number or mix of people. It does require clear intent and the willingness to go through a period of *emptiness* together, wherein no one in the group seeks to be the expert who holds *the answer*, and everyone is consciously open to the wisdom of the group. As Starhawk simply describes it, "Community means strength that joins our strength to do the work that needs to be done. Arms to hold us when we falter. A circle of healing. A circle of friends. Someplace where we can be free" (*Dreaming the Dark* 92). This is a summary of true *community* within the partnership context.

This dream of community, while attainable, is often elusive in an American society based on an agonizing awareness of rank-and-consumption-based competition. Furthermore, many so-called communities that do exist— such as the proliferation of exclusive "gated communities"— are actually based on fragmentation and only identifiable by their ability to keep "others" *out*. This orientation begs the question about how people can see themselves as part of a system or organization if they feel fundamentally separate. These conditions also increase the improbability of realizing a partnership community, and point once again to the need for a fundamental re-visioning and shift in the culture.

As mythologist Jean Houston asserts, "We need models of a new order of relationship and their place in a possible society." That "new order" would be formed in such a way that the society becomes "one in which male and female, science and spirituality, economics and ecology, civic participation and personal growth come together in an integral and interdependent matrix for the benefit of all" (*Jump Time* 14). This integrative vision represents a seeming conundrum, when one of the hallmarks of the Americentric, *power-over* system is the insistence that the white, male, scientific, and Judeo-Christian sources hold all the "correct" keys to governance, economics, social policies, education, and religion. Yet once that paradigm of separation and exclusion is rejected as the "only" or the "always right" model, the way is opened to explore and potentially adopt models and strategies from other groups and other cultures. Indeed, there is a need for innovative processes and designs that are more than mere repetitions of past Americentric models; the shift to partnership communities requires more than "new wine in old skins."

Intercultural Community Models

Local efforts are having increasingly global interactions and impacts. According to Harvard religious studies professor Diana Eck, America is rapidly becoming the most culturally and religiously pluralistic society on earth. Due to those trends, there is a concurrent, growing need for expanding and integrating intercultural understanding, relationships, and leadership styles in order to achieve maximum societal, organizational and personal effectiveness. Intercultural elements are interwoven with one's personal view of the world: how and why things work the way they do, and what is most important. Intercultural epistemologist Dorothy Pennington, in the *Handbook for*

International and Intercultural Communication notes, "Worldview plays a part in determining one's interpersonal power and influence." She warns of the dangers of linking power and influence with ethnocentrism, particularly relative to efforts to promote partnerships, noting, "Dogmatism can occur from cultural myopia, wherein one is unaware of the possibility of differences" (273). When that unawareness or outright dismissal of other's views occurs, extended competition, discrimination, and fragmentation become the order of the day, and any semblance of achieving either community or partnership is disrupted.

By promoting positive, *power-with* images of groups where everyone manifests personal leadership in non-competitive and diverse expressions, there is an opportunity to collectively mend the broken web of our fragmented communities with intercultural, intergenerational, and collaborative efforts. Then those who were previously considered *others* can be valued for their unique perspectives and the wisdom of their experience. These new leaders can then be called to act in service—as stewards and mentors—of the interdependent community and its resources.

In that light, there are threads that can be woven into the American cultural fabric from a variety of other cultural traditions that offer valuable contributions to this exploration of alternative, collaborative belief systems. The intent in their inclusion is to discover principles of inclusiveness and potential models that can assist American organizations in the development of partnerships. I have chosen to focus on the African American and Native American traditions, since they represent groups that have been particularly, historically targeted and discriminated against by the American *power-over* system, and because they offer distinctly different models of relating. The challenge is for an Americentric society addicted to materialism and control to accept alternative, non-Americentric approaches and then apply these principles as appropriate to help effectively manage transitions away from rigid models of competition, domination, and control and toward cultural transformations that are both healing and liberating for all people.

One of the most revered American values is individualism, or the right to live uniquely and to express oneself apart from others. This value is so strong in American culture that at times it seems inimical to hopes of finding *common ground*, creating partnerships, and building community. As Dagara medicine man Malidoma Patrice Somé observes, "The urge for community in the West is challenged by the tendency to see community as antithetical, and even a threat, to individuality" (91). Never having truly experienced a sense of deep community, many Americans fear losing their sense of self in a sea of faceless *others*. Yet as Somé recalls, "I have found that modern people long for the fulfilling connections that are available through a healthy community, the sense of connection and coherence that I have experienced in village life" (91). This is a modern American paradox, captured by Wheatley's observation, "The great missing conversation is about why and how we might be together" (*The Promise and Paradox of Community* 4). Consequently, we have great American cities, but very few true communities.

When individualism is drawn away from ideologies of competition for material progress, it no longer stands in contradiction to partnership, but is essential to it. The *power-over* system co-opted individualism almost as quickly as it appeared as a distinct philosophy of human freedom, and it used it to divide people and create what we now casually refer to as "target markets," "voter pools," or even distinct "faith traditions." Yet when individuals have united across boundaries for a common cause—such as response to the attacks of September 11, 2001, or to the enormously devastating effects of the giant earthquake and tsunami on

December 26, 2004 in southeast Asia—they often report *not* a loss of self, but a greater expression of it through their collective efforts providing service to others. Therein lies the complementary promise of partnership and individualism.

Within African, African-American, and Afro-Caribbean belief systems, the core values of inclusiveness (for all beings and different ways of being) and community are to this day—where they have not been overwhelmed by Americentric individualism—held in the context of interdependence and deep spirituality. Professor John Smith explains, "From childhood, most African Americans are taught verbally and nonverbally just how their actions influence and impact the whole community and ethnic race" (113). Researchers Bell, Bouie, and Baldwin also report that behind the superficial, colonially imposed values, "Cultural values consistent with the basic principles of the African-American worldview are interdependence, cooperation, unity, mutual responsibility, and reconciliation" (54).

Where these indigenous values have survived and been expressed in daily life, the resulting belief system is built around a "both/and" partnership: with the gods, with nature, and with each other. Thus members of Afro-Caribbean communities that I experienced as a Peace Corps Volunteer in Honduras presented a tightly knit extended family system where children were cared for by a wide range of family members and friends, where the community banded together to help care for someone who was seriously ill or had suffered a tragic loss, and where the relationships within the community group were as richly varied and colorful as the spicy ethnic cuisine that was their trademark. If children misbehaved, they were chastised with "Don't portray yourself as poorly raised," which was to bring shame upon the family and the community. While many members of the community were officially either Catholic or "Evangélicos," they also believed in many nature-based gods from ancient traditions, and had woven them into their blended faith tradition. Rather than separation, theirs was an experience of interdependence and integration.

The challenge is to nourish these partnership and community values and share them across traditional boundaries. Somé emphasizes that within his native tradition, "We cannot allow some among us to evolve while some are left behind, because that is not community. Community is the common handling of the journey" (78). This worldview is not solely reflecting the memory of some pre-colonial past; it is the underlying philosophy that informs the decisions and actions of his Dagara tribe *to this day*. Indeed, within this frame of reference, it really does "take a whole village to raise a child" (Smith 113). This core philosophy of fundamental interdependence is also reflected in the ancient African proverb: *I am because we are, and because we are, I am.*

Native American cultures also have a long history of working in harmony with each other and with the earth. Anthropologist Joseph Epes Brown, in *The Spiritual Legacy of the American Indian* describes the experience within shamanically based native cultures. He explains, "Unlike the conceptual categories of Western culture, American Indian traditions do not fragment experience into mutually exclusive dichotomies, but tend rather to stress modes of interrelatedness across categories of meaning, never losing sight of an ultimate wholeness" (71). Although the original sources and ideologies are largely ignored, some of the guiding principles established for the young American nation were borrowed from the integrated system of the "Iroquois," or as they call themselves, the Haudenosaunee, or "people of the longhouse."

The Haudenosaunee confederacy was comprised of six nations: the Onandagas, the Cayugas, the Senecas, the Mohawks, the Oneidas, and the Tuscaroras, and its founding has been established at 1142 C.E. (Wagner 84). This model of cooperating, sovereign nations who had previously warred against each other was an inspiration to the framers of the United States Constitution as they sought to design a new nation, founded on principles of democracy (Wagner 15). This aspect within the establishment of the American body politic is not widely taught, nor is it generally celebrated in Thanksgiving traditions that focus on Native American gifts of food that helped early settlers survive their first harsh winter. The Native American gifts to the settlers proved to be much more far-reaching and fundamental than a celebratory meal, however well received and appreciated.

Within the search for a cultural shift to move beyond the *power-over* constraints that limit the experience of freedom and democracy, the Haudenosaunee example provides a refreshing beacon of hope that together we can create a "completely transformed world." Nowhere is that hope more apparent than in the Haudenosaunee myth of their great, archetypal "Peacemaker," Deganawidah. His was the vision and inspiration (which he accorded to the Great Spirit), the impulse and coordination, and the careful diplomacy that guided the metamorphosis of six distinct nations, from warring tribes to an integrated and peaceful alliance. Jean Houston notes that the story is not only mythic; it also includes elements of historic fact. Deganawidah actually lived, and appeared at a time of great strife and on-going cycles of revenge among the nations that would ultimately form a confederacy under his leadership. He worked with Jigonhsasee, who is considered "the Mother of Nations," and with "the great orator Hayenwatha, remembered as Hiawatha" (*Manual for the Peacemaker* xxi).

Houston reasons that based on the evidence that suggests that the Haudenosaunee influence "extended to the great social theorists of the Enlightenment, among them Montesquieu, Rousseau, and Voltaire" (xxiii); then

"Deganawidah is entitled to be acknowledged as root and inspiration for many of the democracies of the world" (xxiv). This mythos of stepping into the fray as a peacemaker who brings dialogue and healing together with living in harmony on the earth, rather than heavy-handed control that fosters increased enmity and resentment is sorely needed in a world torn apart by war and environmental destruction. It provides inspiration for those who feel called to be the bringers of peace, the creators of community, and the catalysts for change in our world.

Lest anyone seek to dismiss the stories of the Haudenosaunee as the stuff of fairy tales or dead history, Maisie Shenandoah stoutly declares, "I am a Wolf Clan Mother for the Oneida Nation. I have been teaching the traditional ways of the Haudenosaunee, or the Iroquois, for over thirty years" (Wall 132). She carries a dream, passed on from her mother that, "One day we will again stand before the world as a people who have overcome the odds and survived as a nation" (134). Even though many seem to have forgotten, the dream has not died; the "wisdom keepers" carry it on, and keep it alive. One Clan Mother, who chose to remain anonymous, informs photographer and Native American researcher Steve Wall, "Our memories are long, as long as the line of the generations. The elders have always passed on this knowledge. We have been told never to forget. So we remember and pass it on too" (x-xi).

Organizations as Communities

As stated earlier, when faced with the promise and challenges of consciously co-creating community, many Americans dismiss it as wishful thinking. This is particularly true in organizations where there is a long history of hierarchical, authoritarian micro-management. In my role as an organizational consultant, I have encountered many people who do not believe experiencing true community within the organizational setting is even possible. Nevertheless, there are growing numbers of success stories, where the basic organizational culture has been profoundly transformed, and people have been able to build varying degrees of community in their places of work. Wheatley, speaking of her recent work consulting with organizations, reports in *Leadership and the New Science* that the difference in these organizations represents far more than applying new theories and approaches to leadership, or even just thinking about organizations differently. Rather, she observes, "What we were really asking, and what was also being asked of us, was that we change our thinking at the most fundamental level, that of our world view" (171).

The awareness and understanding of the impact of one's own and the collective worldview is of critical importance in making the shift to a partnership organization. I have observed that when organizational partner-members are able to examine collectively the stories that operate in the background (or the *underground*) of their workplaces, coupled with information about other organizations that are succeeding in transforming themselves and experiencing leadership capacity building for everyone, the worldview and organizational culture can indeed be changed.

Changing one's fundamental worldview is not an easy task. I experienced that transformational shift as a Peace Corps Volunteer in Honduras, Central America, when a different perspective of the world than I could have imagined radically expanded my own view of "how things are." For example, my understanding of what it means to truly live in poverty without a safety net was brought home with searing reality as I worked with groups of rural women and young girls for whom a single egg for my cooking demonstration was a precious commodity. My perspectives about the results of Americentric policies on the lives of the majority of the world's "third world" populations, rather than just benefiting the few ruling elites, were forever altered. It was a challenging, chaotic, and life-altering experience. Wheatley contends, "We truly are giving birth to a new worldview," which accounts for some of the chaos we feel (173), and for many it is a parallel to the confusion and paradigm-expanding realities I experienced during my time in Honduras.

Many people are wondering how we can possibly navigate such confusing, ambiguous, and terrifying times. The answer is that we navigate together, in circles and communities that jointly weave new partnerships, and support innovative exploration of new horizons. That navigation and weaving of partnerships also requires new structures, adoption of different models of power and leadership, and the implementation of fundamentally different ways of interacting—some of which are described in this book—than are common in most American organizations today.

Calling the Circle and Holding the Rim

In our lives of rapid change and mobility, many people feel more fragmented and alone in the crowd, and there is a rising hunger for connections that touch us deeper than most superficial workplace or even neighborhood alliances. Perhaps the most difficult and most critical level of change required to realize true partnership and community connections occurs at the level of personal relationships, which is why offering a simple support structure for building community at the interpersonal level is an important consideration. "Calling the circle and holding the rim," a concept introduced by circle leader and trainer Christina Baldwin in *Calling the Circle: The First and Future Culture*, offers an important image of overcoming fragmentation. Any group of people striving to grasp the notion of how they can make a difference in their interactions in the face of sometimes overwhelming obstacles can benefit from its precepts. As Baldwin describes it, when people gather in circles, each one figuratively and consciously "holds the rim" to create a safe space for interacting. That safe space in turn reflects a sacred dimension, which, as Jean Shinoda Bolen suggests, "embodies the collective wisdom of its members" (*Goddesses in Older Women* 179). The image of the circle both encompasses everything that is held within its circumference, and represents a way of being together that is also embracing and supportive of deeper modes of connection, problem solving, and creativity.

Gathering in a circle is itself profoundly symbolic. According to author and anthropologist Angeles Arrien, the circle is an archetypal shape found in the art, architecture, and/or clothing of cultures around the world. She was able to identify that, "In every culture the circle symbolizes wholeness and the experience of unity." This image is particularly important because "When people are engaged in the search for wholeness they aspire to independence and individuation. What they need most is space, room in which to find themselves and develop their own identity" (31). Paradoxically, this is the space created when people gather together in circles for the purpose of telling their stories, engaging in dialogue, and creating community. Ray and Anderson observe, "Elders and story and community—if you dip into one, you draw from another" (310). They urge that as we move from one paradigm to another—from *power-over* to *power-with*—we are in need of "a massive cultural rite of passage." It is during these times of change and transition, as further discussed in chapter 7, that "community could not be more important" (306). The answer to the questions that arise about "Where do we begin, in the move to *power-with* collaborations and partnership communities?" —lies in circle and dialogue processes.

The circle provides the space for *dialogue*, which comes from the Latin words *dia*, meaning, "through" or "with each other," and *logos*, meaning "the word." While humans have apparently been gathering in small groups to talk with each other for millennia, beginning with groupings around the safety and warmth of the campfire, the talking that takes place in *dialogue* is profoundly different from *discussion*, which comes from the Latin word *discutere*, meaning, "to smash to pieces." Given those distinct differences, the circle provides a container for openly inquiring into—yet refraining from judging—another's view.

Thus, discussion is frequently combative, where often participants are rehearsing their responses without really listening to each other as they attempt to prove the other "side" wrong. Discussion, which is closely linked to debate, is based on the assumption that there is only one answer—the "truth," as provided by one side or the other—and the object is to prove who owns it. In their quest to be *right*, the opportunity for experiencing true *community* is often sacrificed. In that context, there may even be *power-over* hierarchies masquerading in circle clothing, wherein, Baldwin warns, there is "hierarchy curled into an innocuous ball to make itself more palatable" (70). In that situation, even organizations with a predisposition to operating in *power-with* find it an elusive aspiration.

Dialogue, on the other hand, is based on the assumption that many people have pieces of the answer, and that together the group can use those pieces to craft a new solution. In *dialogue*, people come together with mutual respect *even when participants disagree*, and they strive for common understanding that is expansive, rather than seeking to "win" or "be right." There is a shared recognition that wisdom is not the sole territory of any one group. According to Martin Buber in *The Knowledge of Man*, dialogue is "a mode of exchange among human beings in which there is a true turning to one another, and a full appreciation of another not as an object in a social function, but as a true human being." The importance of this notion cannot be overstated. William Isaacs, senior lecturer at MIT's Sloan School of Management and Director of The Dialogue Project, notes, "If fragmentation is a condition of our times, then dialogue is one strategy for stepping back from the way of thinking which fragmentation produces" (360). In my experience, unless group members in *any* group can feel safe and accepted and *heard*, achieving an enduring shift in the quality of their relationships and tapping into the deep wisdom of the group is an improbable expectation.

There are many variations of the dialogue circle model that operate in groups around the world, ranging from small informal groups of women in widely divergent countries who are linked through the PeacexPeace organization, to large corporate universities and gatherings of people representing divergent views. For example, I worked with a small private school that holds a weekly morning circle or "council" for all faculty, staff, administrative personnel and students, which they find helps to resolve many potential divisive issues before they escalate. A nonprofit organization calls a circle on Friday afternoons as a way to debrief the week and decompress the frustrations of their crisis-oriented work before they go home to their families and friends. A workshop on "The Spirit of Circle" was recently held on the Microsoft campus in Redmond, Washington, as conveners promised "a fascinating convergence of kitchen table wisdom, bringing heart to the workplace, and learning ways of communicating which cross the divides of diversity." There have also been a variety of dialogue gatherings in recent years based on international, intergenerational, and interfaith coalitions.

At the most basic community level, there are small, informal groups meeting over lunch in workplace conference rooms or in the evenings in rotating co-worker's or neighbor's homes, all of which seek to develop a deeper understanding and foster a sense of community and belonging. In these conversations, often warmed by candles as small representative "campfires" and supplemented by the ancient ceremony of "breaking bread together" over a shared meal, people are overcoming their isolation, opening their hearts, slowing down to really listen to each other, together firming their resolve to make a difference, and finding hope again.

Based on the precepts of Diffusion Theory, Bolen suggests that if enough people regularly gather in circles of community, at the point that the millionth circle is launched, it will be the "tipping point." There will be a cultural shift into an entirely new, "post-patriarchal human era" (*The Millionth Circle* 18). It all hinges on building trust—within a new sense of community—which can be built within interactive circles that eschew domination and control and invite partnership and collaboration.

Partners in the World Community

There was a time when the archetypal rugged American (individualist) pioneer had the luxury of heroically conquering new frontiers without realizing, or caring about, long-term repercussions. This Americentric worldview shunned input from *others*, including indigenous people with a long history and connection to the land, and it was far easier to ignore or not to share input when communication across the new frontier was slow, difficult, and costly.

These days, the consequences resulting from our actions and the feedback of those who have been affected are often immediate and reactionary in our communicatively complex and information-saturated world. There is little question that we have already shifted into a very different world from that of the pilgrims and the pioneers. What threatens to divide us now is not too little shared knowledge, but rather an overwhelming stream of information flowing so quickly and easily that it becomes increasingly difficult to make sense of what holds value, what is unmitigated propaganda, and what is simply noise. Yet in an era of such easy access, information is also paradoxically fodder for increased fragmentation and disenfranchisement, as many large hierarchies become ever more secretive, and control of the media is held by an ever-tightening group of patriarchs.

While we must focus on redefining our own organizational relationships, it is also imperative that we remain aware that those relationships do not exist in isolation from the world at large. In an era when quantum theory has demonstrated the reciprocal relationships of all elements within a system, organizations, whether small local entrepreneurs, publicly funded entities, or vast multi-national conglomerates, have a profound impact on events and populations around the world. Indeed, in these times of ever-increasing communication networks, restlessly mobile populations, cross-referenced global markets, and the success of newly-partnering political alliances such as the European Union, it is ever more critical that the costs and benefits of organizational actions are considered within the context of the entire planetary community.

Yet American economic interests, fueled by centuries of operating from a position of manifest destiny based on alleged moral and cultural superiority, are continuing to exert power that includes providing the impetus for raiding resources, polluting ecosystems, and exploiting populations around the globe. American corporate and political dominance is a heavy weight for smaller, resource-poor nations, whose weaker voices are scarcely heard above the voracious appetite for escalating hegemonic power. Nevertheless, U.S. consumers, many of whom are blithely unaware of its systemic connection within their own country, do not understand how their bottomless consumption of material goods at Wal-Mart, which leads the charge among giant discount superstores, has resulted in the closing of local businesses because a smaller retailer cannot compete on price or even a larger manufacturer can no longer supply Wal-Mart with goods more cheaply than those manufactured in sweatshops overseas, particularly in China. Ironically, just as American economic and military might are creating dependencies around the globe, so too Wal-Mart and a select group of other multi-national conglomerates are eliminating competitors and thus creating trade imbalances and dependencies within the American economy while China is quietly, steadily increasing its share of the global market.

The Japanese *kanji*, or alphabet symbol, for *opportunity* is comprised of the symbols for *trouble* and *gathering crisis*. Similarly, within the current global crises lies both challenge and opportunity. Deep, divisive wounds must be addressed by visionary leadership that is both personal and partnering, which does not abdicate responsibility for holding the center in a world of uncertainty. We simultaneously face a myriad of painful global crises and an immense spiritual opening that requires us to live and lead at a higher, more informed and aware level. We have the power and the responsibility to operate in partnership, both among ourselves and with other nations and people of the entire world. It is time we both step away from narrow definitions of "truth" that feed *power-over* dominance, and provide leadership that is based in the stewardship of diverse cultures and the earth we call home.

You must be the change you wish to see in the world.
        Mahatma Gandhi

⚙ Chapter 7 ⚙

Weaving New Patterns and Changing the Story

The case for moving beyond the traditional *power-over* system into a fundamentally different way of operating is compelling. Residual doubts about the need for changes in the ways we operate are shaken loose by deep and reverberating tragedies of wars, economic deprivation, social unrest, and environmental degradation. There is no longer comfort in secure complacency, which harbors in its place only defensiveness, fear, and confusion. World leaders and individuals alike have been jolted into frightening and uncharted territory. Traditional patriarchal *power-over* models and strong-arm strategies may remind us of past triumphs, but are increasingly ineffective at tackling the mounting tragedies they machined. Yet, authoritarian leaders in government agencies, private nonprofit organizations, and corporations alike employ over and over again these same failed strategies in the face of diminishing returns, all the while expecting different results.

Partnership finds seed when those with imagination are inspired to shed complacency, confront their fear and doubts about the status quo, and trust their intuition that they are not alone in their hope and determination to craft a better world. Moving beyond the *power-over* system into partnerships requires immense changes in both relationships and organizational structures, ranging from individual, interpersonal relationships through organizational norms and international diplomatic strategies. Turning away from the status quo and moving in the direction of those changes requires a courageous, growing company of visionary pioneers committed to co-creating partnerships. This concluding chapter addresses the challenges and patterns of the transitional journey, reflected by mythic examples.

Weaving New Visions and Mental Models

One of the most difficult things to accomplish for many people is to make a mid-stream course correction. At some point in our social and cultural development, we adopt an image or mental model of how things *should* work in order to achieve our preferred outcomes. Then we direct all of our efforts toward making those images or dreams come true, or at least toward seeing that that is the only way for them to be true. In the organizational context, we are told to "plan your work and work your plan," or "work smarter," or "trim the sails," all in pursuit of the "bottom-line," or the ultimate goal of monetary gain for the organization and supposedly for the worker, as well.

When faced with challenges, rather than re-evaluate the organizational mission, motives, and methods, many managers will simply design new selling points for the old goals and shuffle or discard staff members. Management then pumps up the motivational rhetoric to ensure that, as fellow workers are quietly pushed aside, the remaining ones don't lose sight of the "big picture." Often people keep doing the same things they had been doing because they do not have an idea of what else to do, and they fear the ambiguity of the unknown. This pattern exemplifies Einstein's oft-quoted saying that the definition of insanity is doing the same thing again and again while expecting different results. Following this logic, the sane thing is careful reconsideration of alternative paths and desired outcomes.

In this time of massive cultural and technological changes, as individuals and organizations seek alternative paths, Jean Houston expresses the pervasive query, "What must we do to become stewards of our own evolution? What must we do to move ourselves and the world to the next stage?" (*Jump Time* 32). As responsible stewards, if we expect to shift both fundamental processes and desired outcomes in organizations at all levels of our society, what we must do is move beyond superficial window dressing techniques that merely shuffle and tweak existing approaches or entertain the troops for a day. The *underground* and the *battlegrounds* need courageous attention from peacemakers who can rise above narcissistic self-interest in the hope of reaching the *common ground.*

There is a rising chorus that we have lost our way, and our mythos, or the story line of our culture. The melody of the siren's song says to "get back to basics," in order to reclaim the "good old days." The story line carries the narrative threads of things past, the roles and responsibilities of individuals within their communities, and the vision of what might yet be. With only partial, "sound bite" heroic stories as models, some feel a sense of loss and a feeling of being lost: of being endlessly doomed to repeat the same destructive cycles until the earth can no longer sustain human life. This is deeply disturbing for many people, and with good reason. Paul Ray and Sherry Ruth Anderson recall Carl Jung's observation, "When an individual loses his story . . . confusion and disorientation result." Worse yet, "When a people lose their story, the entire culture suffers from strange pathologies" (300). Yet Ray and Anderson warn that endlessly retelling the same stories and clinging to the visions of a golden past can keep us stagnant and "without imagination." They contend, "We *had* to lose [our story], because every age needs its own wisdom" (300). In other words, the time has come to move away from *insanely* repeating the predictable patterns and narrow solutions that are only producing more of the same—competition, chaos, confusion, and the degradation of many life support systems —while expecting different results.

Some are already beginning to carefully pick the timeworn strands of ancient myths and weave them into the material of modern life, tracing the imprints of heroes and patriarchs while seeking to "move the myth forward." In the process of that tracing, it is apparent that we are in need of a newly woven story, starting with a new systemic warp, then adding fresh weft threads, newly creative and distinctively patterned designs, and the wisdom gained from past experiences, triumphs, and mistakes. But where is the pattern for the weave, or the map for the journey? Healer David La Chapelle, in *Navigating the Tides of Change* notes, "A map is a memory of what has been explored, a description of what is known" (10). In ancient times, the maps were constantly evolving, as new lands were explored, unknown inhabitants were encountered, and more accurate mapping methods were developed. So, too, we are called to embark on a journey into lands where others have lived before, yet they are relatively unknown in Americentric story lines. Our maps and our story are evolving as new information and deeper understanding becomes available.

Just as Robert Frost famously mused over "two roads" that "diverged in a yellow wood," we stand at a threshold, needing to take steps into the unknown toward uncertain new beginnings, while simultaneously struggling with the fear and inertia that often keep us attached to the status quo. Baldwin urges, "We need a revolution in the West. Not a violent overthrow, but a re-evolution, a willingness to take responsibility for the course of history that is being set forth through our compliance" (76). We need heroes who come full circle, and return from their dark nights and challenges to become fully engaged in their communities. We need elders to hold the container for the young heroes who are facing their trials, and to provide wisdom that is expansive and encouraging, rather than self-gratifying authority that is diminishing and domineering.

In spite of the insecurity of the times, Houston urges movement noting, "When we get beyond the shutterings of our local cultural trance, we gain the courage to nurture the emerging forms of the possible human and the possible society" (*Jump Time* 10). Outworn models that in essence define who we are and thereby limit our potential, also trap us in automatic, reactive responses. Thus we are called to the quest to replace traditional images with new descriptions of the "possible human and the possible society" within a partnership framework. We are called to explore the "road less traveled."

There are emerging opportunities to imagine fresh new visions, and to weave collectively a new cultural fabric wherein the threads exist in balanced reciprocity. Ray and Anderson suggest that new designs are arising from a myriad of players: the "story-listeners, story-evokers, artists and teachers of every sort who can call forth the stories we need now" (300). Just as Southern California suffered disastrous wild fires in the autumn of 2003, which were followed by bright new shoots, sprouting amid blackened stumps and ash, so too there are signs of movement in our culture. True, there is despair at the seemingly endless cycle of fear and revenge and the destructive *power-over* maneuverings of corporate interests, coupled with a reactive impulse to strengthen the current system by restricting civil liberties, ratcheting down the opportunities for teachers to do what they do best—all in the interest of "leaving no child behind"—while heroically bombing the "evil-doers." Yet there are also people who are committed to taking "the road less traveled" by collectively developing new structures, processes, and answers to complex problems.

As a nation, we are not only in the chaotic jumble of multiple changes; we are in the "between" space of transition; the old ways no longer sustain us, and new ways have not yet taken root. Within that open expanse, Ray and Anderson point out, "A space has been cleared for innovation and creativity" (301). Into this opening a group that does not yet know it is a group is emerging—the group

Ray and Anderson have named the *Cultural Creatives*. They declare, "Everywhere that harbingers of a new mythos are appearing, *Cultural Creatives* are leading the way" (301). Part of the enormous challenge facing those who seek to re-weave American society is the formidable task of bringing this group together—which may take the form of numerous small groups "webbed" together—not to melt them into unified anonymity, but to strengthen their sense of numbers and community and collective potential. A sense of community and identity will in turn strengthen their resolve and invigorate their impact in the midst of *power-over* intrigues that include increasingly limited access to what was once considered public information and to American media outlets, skewed reporting of both national and global events, and brutal harassment of those who have the temerity to protest their policies.

This transition has already proven to be a difficult passage, and there are more difficulties ahead as we move through successive cycles of change. It is important to remember that we do not have constantly to react to the crises of our time; we can be proactive participants, designing a new cultural fabric. Marilyn French suggests, "The idea that we can transform the world may seem utopian, idealistic, or just simple-minded. ... The world will change anyway. It is not inconceivable that humans themselves can participate in forming the direction of that change" (544). Just as the Buddhists speak of "dependent co-arising," wherein the movement of every element affects every other element in a system, Margaret Wheatley emphasizes, "We inhabit a world that co-evolves as we interact with it" (9), and she assures us, "The world is not an independently existing thing. It's a complex, never still, always weaving tapestry" (*Leadership and the New Science* 39). In that respect, we can have an impact and a responsibility in the trajectory of transformation. Even though the changes are mounting and the outcomes cannot be assured, there is an age-old, yet ever-evolving map for the transition process, and there are guides for the journey.

Weaving the Wilderness

I am participating in the creation of yet another culture, a new story to explain the world and our participation in it, a new value system with images and symbols that connect us to each other and the planet. (Anzaldúa 380)

We are living in the midst of rapid, constant changes, which in turn require nonstop, over-lapping transitions. The pace and scope of these changes and transitions, occurring at all levels of our lives, often require different approaches than the processes that worked twenty—or even ten—years ago. Houston calls this the "jump time," which indicates "a whole system in transition, a condition of interactive change that affects every aspect of life as we know it" (*Jump Time* 11). That constant upheaval and the difficulty in carving out retreat, or "re-creation" time are sources of great stress for many individuals, and they are not alone. The accelerating pace of change and the multitude of widely varying changes have tipped the fragile sense of continuity and stability in core cultural infrastructures, and stress-related illnesses are the leading causes of death in the United States. Yet while watching the old structures disintegrate is frightening, there is also hope in that it provides opportunities for new forms, relationships, and realities to arise. Therein lies the prospect that this era could become both a mythic transition and part of a culture-wide and even global initiation into a wholly different way of being in the world.

Some believe that the very openness and instability of transition offer an opportunity for creative changes that did not exist even a few years ago. A similar situation presented itself to the city leaders of Santa Barbara, California, when the 1925 earthquake destroyed much of downtown. At that time, a few respected, visionary leaders pressed for making conscious choices regarding an architectural theme that had not existed before. Indeed, it would have been difficult, if not impossible before the earthquake presented a virtually blank slate for them to change the "operating system" and create a beautiful, architecturally cohesive city. So, too, visionary leaders in these times are speaking in favor of instituting conscious changes in the social fabric and architecture of American culture, even as fear of failing systems is entering the public discourse and prompting either frantic efforts to shore up old programs or deceptive proposals for radical changes that would benefit the few at the expense of the many.

Some of the fundamental changes—which will in turn bring about transitions—are explored in this work. While multiple examples have been provided where at least some partnership elements have been successfully woven into the organizational structure and psyche, they are by no means widespread at this time. There is an enormous need to make the fundamental move from a *power-over* system based on "rankism" to one based on partnership. As discussed in earlier chapters, this will require large-scale shifting from predominantly top-down management styles of leadership to stewardship and service models embedded in flatter, more participative organizations. Other changes that ripple out from this emerging vision, which will be covered in future books, include:

• Moving beyond the dominance of the hero and the patriarch, and bringing different archetypes to the fore, which promote healing the rifts between the masculine and feminine and between humankind and the natural world, thereby re-mythologizing our worldview.

• Radically changing the prevailing perspectives about both the young, new members and the older, more experienced members of an organization and of society.

A Model for the Transitional Journey

Many traditional, indigenous cultures recognize that transitional times, whether in the life of an individual or the life of the tribe, represent both particular challenges and important opportunities for growth. Within their worldview, initiation rituals or "rites of passage" supported individuals traversing unknown, unpredictable territory into a "new life."

Anthropologists Arnold Van Gennep and Victor Turner first documented those indigenous rituals. Van Gennep, in his 1909 classic *Les Rites de Passage*, identified and published the common structure and specific stages in the traditional rites of passage conducted in many different cultures. He realized that ancient people constructed rites that reflected the biological processes they experienced throughout their lives, and he named the stages of their rites separation, margin, and aggregation. Subsequently, Turner, in *The Ritual Process: Structure and Anti-Structure* published in 1969, focused on the "betwixt and between," or liminal period woven into the core of those rites. Both researchers support the thesis that rites of passage and initiations provide clear markers for an individual's initiatory move from one stage of life to another (Mahdi 5). Building on the work of van Gennep and Turner, other theorists have extrapolated the indigenous initiation process to organizations, cultural groups, and the entire world, all of which appear to be in flux, and at a faster pace than ever before.

It is now understood that initiation and ritual comprise an ancient wisdom tradition for coping with changes and transitions. Ray and Anderson note that in traditional societies "changes that could be cataclysmic for the individual and the community were woven into the fabric of life so that each change was meaningful and connected" (251). Thus, within indigenous cultures, everyone operated within a cooperative construct that provided narratives, direction, and meaning for life's journey (Flinders, *At the Root of This Longing* 251). This container supported both surface-level changes, and deep transformation—for the individual, the organization, or the culture ready to make fundamental changes. Humanities professor Bruce Lincoln, in *Emerging from the Chrysalis* observes, "Most rites of passage . . . do what they claim to do: they transform people." Furthermore, he extends that effect, noting that some groups believe that within "rites of renewal . . . the cosmos itself is transformed along with the initiand" (6). All of these researchers have sought to identify the elements of successful human transformation, hoping to learn how that achievement can be replicated. The challenge for our times is to make our transformations consciously without yielding to old habits that do little more than circle back to worn out dogma.

In my work as an organizational consultant, I have encountered that many people awash in a sea of transition find it helpful to learn that there is a normal and natural process for traversing transitions. Based on the work of van Gennep and Turner, organizational consultant and transition theorist William Bridges developed a model, widely used for more than fifteen years, that also encompasses three stages: *endings*, the *neutral zone* or *wilderness*, and *new beginnings*. It has been applied in many modern, non-ritualized transitions to help people understand and manage the dynamics of shifting from one place, pattern, or process to another, and to ensure that desired changes take place.

Understanding the transition process is particularly important because, while many people focus on specific changes as the culprits for their discomfort, Bridges contends, "It isn't the changes that do you in. It's the transitions." He explains that change is the *external* situation, whereas transition is the *internal*, "psychological *process* people go through to come to terms with the new situation" (*Managing Transitions* 3). In other words, transition is the re-orientation that people go through as they shift from what-has-been to what-is-going-to-be. This is a critical distinction; for, as Bridges notes, even if the change is implemented, "Without transition, a change is mechanical, superficial, empty" (*The Way of Transition* 3). Whereas most people focus on the implementation of changes, the transition process itself is crucial because, he emphasizes, "Unless transition occurs, change will not work" (*Managing Transition* 4). When a change process is implemented but the transition is not fully accomplished, many people wind up feeling further confused, taken advantage of, and perhaps more adamantly opposed to changes in general. There are many examples of failed institutional changes. As Wheatley points out, "Senior corporate leaders report that up to 75% of their change projects do not yield the promised results" (*Leadership and the New Science* 138). While there is no single reason for that shocking rate of failure, clearly old strategies and solutions are not working, and it is important to transform how organizations deal with change itself.

This is where understanding the transition process and having some sense of managing it—through all of its stages—is immensely helpful. Ironically, a transition *starts with an ending*, which usually involves some sense of loss, and brings with it feelings of grief (even when the change is anticipated and desired). Then before the new beginnings (phase three) can be fully entered, there is a "kind of emotional wilderness," an ambiguous space that is neither the old reality nor yet fully the new. Bridges calls this phase the "neutral zone" or the "wilderness," and notes that it is crucial that it be traversed (*Managing Transitions* 5). He declares that this wilderness "is both a dangerous and an opportune place, and it is the very core of the transition process." Although many people would prefer to skip the wilderness, Bridges cautions, "People make the new beginning only if they have first made an ending and spent some time in the neutral zone/*wilderness*" (6). For all its chaos and confusion, the wilderness passage is critical.

Thus, similar to the classic hero's journey, a successful transitional — and transformational — journey requires casting off one's accustomed moorings and moving away from familiar shores. As writer André Gide suggests, "One doesn't discover new lands without consenting to lose sight of the shore for a very long time." Nonetheless, losing sight of familiar shores is at the very least disconcerting, and can provoke fear of being lost in a wilderness without map, markers, or compass.

Quite appropriately, this separation is followed by a passage through a wilderness that can be compared to the mythic descent experience, wherein one is required to face the monsters and demons of their deepest fears. Docking at new shores and bringing the gifts acquired through one's *wilderness* learning to the residents of the new land conclude the heroic, transitional journey. Many, when forced to let go of past structures, are eager to skip any sense of an ambiguous "in-between," and immediately plug in to the latest trend and newest solution, wrongly thinking that they know a shortcut. Yet experiencing both endings and wilderness is essential for individuals, for organizations, and for entire societies, if they truly expect to cast off from old "shores" and fully realize the massive paradigm shifts required for realizing truly new beginnings and finding new lands.

When endings have been fully acknowledged and grieved, and the liminal space of the wilderness has been successfully navigated, the traveler is ready to commence with new beginnings. Bridges cautions that beginnings are not the same as starts. "Starts involve new situations. Beginnings involve new understandings, new values, new attitudes, and—most of all—new identities" (*Managing Transitions* 50). As discussed earlier, when the learnings of one's personal odysseys are retained and fully integrated into the fabric of an individual, organizational, or cultural life, the ability to move forward and begin anew is profoundly enhanced.

A Caterpillar's End of the World

The transitional journey is similar to the profound metamorphosis experienced by the monarch butterflies that migrate each winter to a grove behind my home. I have been told by visiting biologists that when the caterpillar enters its chrysalis, it turns to "mush" before it is reconstituted as a beautiful butterfly. Creationist Evolution Biologist Elisabet Sahtouris offers more details:

> My favorite metaphor for the current world transition, first pointed out to me by Norie Huddle, is that of a butterfly in metamorphosis. It goes like this: A caterpillar crunches its way through its ecosystem, cutting a swath of destruction by eating as much as hundreds of times its weight in a day, until it is too bloated to continue and hangs itself up, its skin then hardening into a chrysalis. Inside this chrysalis, deep in the caterpillar's body, tiny things biologists call 'imaginal disks' begin to form. Not recognizing the newcomers, the caterpillar's immune system snuffs them as they arise. But they keep coming faster and faster, then linking up with each other. Eventually the caterpillar's immune system fails from the stress and

the disks become imaginal cells that build the butterfly by feeding on the soupy meltdown of the caterpillar's body. It took a long time for biologists to understand the reason for the immune system attack on the incipient butterfly cells, but eventually they discovered that the butterfly has its own unique genome, carried by the caterpillar, inherited from long ago in evolution, yet not part of it as such. If we see ourselves as imaginal discs working to build the butterfly of a better world, we will understand that we are launching a new genome to replace that of the current unsustainable system. We will also see how important it is to link with each other in the effort, to recognize how many different kinds of imaginal cells it will take to build a butterfly with all its capabilities and colors. (Personal correspondence, 3/19/05)

Many people report similar feelings of liquefaction as they undergo initiations and transformation. They feel as if they have to disintegrate, surrendering their individuality in some way, and can no longer claim their previous identity, nor have they achieved a new state; they are "betwixt and between." As Hollis observes, "The butterfly, like the soul, is obliged to go through transformative stages before it can attain that fragile, elusive beauty for which it is destined" (85). Likewise, both individuals and organizations have to surrender their grasp of some long-favored, tried-and-true systems in order to fully move into a new way of being in the world.

Even when all seems lost, the "imaginal disks" appear, and act as catalysts for a metamorphosis. Ray and Anderson suggest that within organizations and the culture at large, the *Cultural Creatives* are the imaginal disks in these times of massive change (272). Yet many *Cultural Creatives* report feeling as if they are the "odd ducks" in their organizations, and feel they are in danger—similar to the earliest imaginal cells in the nascent butterfly—of being suppressed or excluded by an organizational or cultural immune system that cannot tolerate "foreign bodies." This indicates a need to consciously seek out others who are ready to develop partnerships, so they can nourish each other and the metamorphosis can be completed.

A remarkable story of unlikely partnerships and long-term perseverance by a growing company of "imaginal cells" has produced a permanent sanctuary for those fragile over-wintering monarchs behind my home. Forty years of on-going efforts by a variety of concerned local groups and originally unrelated individuals to prevent development of the land near the monarch grove and the neighboring vernal pools finally resulted in an impressive community partnership. A coalition of representatives from the city of Goleta, Santa Barbara County, the University of California, Santa Barbara (UCSB), and the owners of the land carefully developed a proposal for a complex land exchange coupled with a large (over $20 million) settlement payment.

The hard work and dedication of a legion of volunteers, public servants, and individuals who clustered together in a variety of initiatives was required to complete the necessary agreements, raise the money, and attain approval of the California Coastal Commission. Their efforts created the synergy that produced a win-win solution and a collaborative fundraising effort that felt like a miracle to those who had worked for so long to prevent development and preserve the land. They realized that although there had been many discouraging events along the way, and their experiences with an earlier developer had felt insulting, devious, and manipulative, all of those so-called negative instances had in fact served to catalyze their determination, and to energize and lend inspiration to their efforts. When the Ellwood Mesa land cleared escrow and was dedicated as public open space in February 2005, there was a celebration of both the preservation of a unique ecosystem and of the successful partnering of many people who might never have met without the *common ground* of their love for the land and their willingness to dedicate countless hours to the cause.

This kind of long-term collaboration requires a trust that the knowledge of what to do in the face of seemingly insurmountable obstacles, and that the wisdom to birth or "midwife" that knowledge, lies deep within the psyche of those who will attune themselves to its messages and enter into co-creative partnerships. There lies the hope in leaving the patriarchal, *power-over* shores; together we can find new land: a land where freedom, equality, dignity, and respect, when released from competition and control, can bloom in fertile partnership soil.

Mythic Transition Metaphors

Odysseus (of *The Odyssey*), Parsifal (of the Grail myth), Adam and Eve (of Genesis), and the Israelites (of Exodus) each spent time in the "wilderness" of transition, which is variously represented by the sea, the forest, the desert, or some nebulous place outside the "garden." Odysseus begins his twenty-year sojourn with the conquest of Troy, and continues through a wide range of challenges, which take place either on the sea or on islands. Parsifal traverses the forest, sometimes seeming to travel in circles before he succeeds in finding the Grail Castle. Adam and Eve are exiled from the only home they have known, and sent out into an unknown expanse—the wilderness of ambiguity and the world of work. The Israelites wander in the barren desert seeking the "promised land." Odysseus's, Parsifal's, and the Israelites' wilderness journeys are particularly instructive for the trials they entail.

It is important to understand that the transitional wilderness of "betwixt and between" can occur when one consciously makes the leap from the past, or it can be thrust upon one unbidden and unprepared. In other words, the organization may gradually outgrow its structure and policies, or it may be forced to respond to sudden shifts in market dynamics or workforce composition, such as a marked increase in the range of employees' diversity, with subsequent needs for developing multicultural understanding. Either way, it requires what Jung calls "holding the tension," or the paradoxes of tenacity and flexibility, and of vulnerability and bravery. Likewise, many people feel pushed or pulled into a transition that they did not consciously choose. They may have felt quite content with the status quo, or they may have disliked conditions as they were, but resisted a particular change because it created a resonance with painful past experiences. Then, when they finally do enter into the transition process, their worst fears are sometimes confirmed.

Odysseus and Parsifal. Odysseus, who originally resisted his "call," provides a classic example of what Bridges terms a "reactive" transition; one in which the change occurs first, and then transition results. Actually, Bridges notes that sometimes "even the prospect of change can put us in transition" (*The Way of Transition* 3-4). After finally yielding to his call, Odysseus had ample opportunities to experience distressing aspects of the ending (first) phase in his transitional, transformational journey. Not only did he reluctantly leave behind his wife and infant son, but as Houston notes, "at every stage and with every loss, Odysseus and his men mourn the crewmates who have been wrecked or drowned or eaten by monsters." For modern applications, she observes, "So must we grieve as we make the journey of transformation through our lives, for the parts of ourselves that are shorn away or engulfed by our experiences need and deserve to be named, mourned, and remembered" (*The Hero and the Goddess* 211).

Admittedly, grieving is not commonly encouraged in Americentric organizations. Yet I have observed that if grieving and acknowledgement of loss are not allowed, those feelings are suppressed, finding refuge in the organizational "shadow," and then surfacing from time to time in seemingly unprovoked angry outbursts or sabotage. On the other hand, this is not to suggest that individuals stay indefinitely in that grieving space, since for some that attitude can itself become an addictive trap. These are the folks who maintain a focus on past wounds and injustices, resisting all attempts to introduce alternate perspectives, relinquish victim mentality, and move forward. They often need someone to help them understand that their addiction to receiving attention and wallowing in self-pity is not helping either the organization or themselves.

Parsifal provides another model of the transitional figure, one whose ending occurred when he willingly chose to leave behind his sheltered home. Although he was sorry to leave his mother, he was so intrigued by the possibilities of knighthood that he felt compelled to depart, and ventured forth intrepidly, drawn to his own version of "betwixt and between," neither *here* nor fully *there*.

This kind of transition is a "developmental" transition, which, Bridges explains, "is not triggered by an external change but is produced by a natural, inner unfolding of those aspects of ourselves that are built right into who we are and how we are made" (*The Way of Transition* 5). Examples of common developmental transitions include adolescence and the mid-life movement from adult to senior citizen (which may or may not include an initiation into elderhood). Many people experience the urge to evolve in ways they had not foreseen, or even consciously selected. They feel an unnamed compulsion to shift some aspect of their lives, and at some level (consciously or unconsciously) fear dire consequence if the change is not made. Likewise, at this critical time on planet earth, Houston observes, "never has the ultimatum 'grow or die' threatened us more" (*The Hero and the Goddess* 29). We are challenged to allow the death of parts of ourselves or of our society that no longer serve us, while also supporting the mourning of their loss, in order to fully let go and move to the next phase of our collective journey(s) of transformation.

"Reactive" and "developmental" transitions are not always so neatly discerned. Sometimes, one leads to the other, as Bridges reports in his own experience through the extended illness and eventual death of his wife, "A developmental transition led to a change, and that change led to a reactive transition" (*The Way of Transition* 13). This set of processes can be particularly disconcerting for those who are in some way interdependent with the person in transition, and can lead to confusion and guilt feelings for everyone. People sometimes wonder what they could have done to affect a different outcome, and feel guilty because they did not *do* something to make things easier. Furthermore, developmental transitions are particularly challenging in that people do not generally plan for them, are not always aware they are evolving, and often do not have a clear sense of where to go next.

Unfortunately, many people feel that in order to let go of their prior situation, they must somehow make it be wrong, and subsequently attempt to divorce themselves completely from this "wrong" situation. Bridges cautions, "Transition does not require that you reject or deny the importance of your old life, just that you let go of it" (*The Way of Transition* 16). No doubt the old life had served some important functions for the past level of development.

Letting go can be tricky. It does not necessarily mean physically leaving (e.g., resigning from the job, getting a divorce, moving to a new town); rather it means letting go of the old *relation* to that particular situation. No matter what the impetus, letting go can be a difficult act. Sometimes we cling to old patterns, relationships, and stories with all our might; other times we distract ourselves from the necessity of letting go by creating a life full of constant changes, which preclude having to do the much harder work of integrating transitions. As I have worked with groups around the country, I have had various people tell me they are "always in transition," but as they described their situation, it became clear that they were in fact avoiding transition, and in activating that escape mechanism, had in the process become addicted to change.

Change addicts may feel that making the deep, inner changes required by transition would force them to look foolish relative to beliefs they had previously held about themselves, others, or some situation in the larger society or the world. Their sense of "truth" or even "reality" may feel uncomfortably compromised. Then, as Bridges cites the Russian novelist Leo Tolstoy, because those elements have "been woven thread by thread into the fabric of their lives," they may feel as if their lives are coming unraveled (*The Way of Transition* 17). The sense of loss is both deep and disturbing. Bridges acknowledges it may "be hooked into archetypal fantasies of being expelled from the human contact of the village or the tribe and doomed to wander as an outcast" (*The Way of Transition* 60). The fear of being banished from "the garden" casts a long shadow. No wonder many people fear and resist transition. When it involves something as fundamental and enormous as moving from the patriarchal, *power-over* system into partnership, a lot is at stake.

After *endings*, with attendant losses and mourning, people enter the *wilderness*, which many experience as feeling lost and perhaps abandoned. The familiar boundaries and shores are no longer in place, and the individual or organization feels surrounded by the unknown. Hollis echoes the lament: "The old authorities have lost their power and the maps are missing" (109). The individual may experience cycles of clear seeing chased by vague contemplation and subtle intuitions, dramatic feelings, and dead ends. Regarding the often-confusing and uncomfortable concept of transitional wilderness, Jungian analyst Wolfgang Giegerich explains, "Wilderness…is a psychological mode of being-in-the-world or a logical status in which life and world are viewed. It is anywhere where relentless self-exposure to the unknown in its infinity and with its unpredictability takes place" (206). Ambiguity reigns supreme.

For individuals who were raised within the American culture—steeped in dualism (which often limits choices to "here" or "there"), taught the high value of completion, and seasoned with a low tolerance for ambiguity— this is by far the most frightening phase of the transition process. Many find they are unprepared for the double nature of the *wilderness* passage, in that it encompasses both a loss that may feel like death and the promise of new beginnings. Ray and Anderson explain, "It is a death space where the initiate's old sense of self is undone and dissolved. And it is also a rich and fertile openness where the old elements of self are transmuted into new patterns" (269). Unable to comprehend the "both/and" nature of the situation, many people find themselves at a loss for where to turn and how to be self-determining when they fail to grasp new parameters or ground rules.

Indeed, for many individuals, the journey from *power-over* to partnership will take place in the midst of what may feel like chaos, and perhaps even anarchy, for those who crave predictability and a sense of stability. There may be an increased "backlash" effect by some who call ever more loudly to get "back to basics," which can result in startling reactions like willingly surrendering civil liberties traditionally held inviolable. There may also be a rise in ethnocentric and xenophobic behaviors, as people experience waves of "culture shock" or "transition shock" (Kim; Bennett; Gannon). All of this will require particular attention and support.

Odysseus was the classic wilderness wanderer, haplessly encountering one challenging obstacle after another in his on-going quest to return home to Ithaca. Parsifal also had times of feeling lost in the forest — often a metaphor for the unconscious — meeting his own version of enemy knights and dragons to be vanquished. Adam and Eve no doubt endured fear and confusion as they transitioned from the peaceful, bountiful "garden" to an adulthood of trials and tribulations. Each had a unique set of ordeals and obstacles to face, which reminds us, as psychologist Joseph Henderson and anthropologist Maud Oakes observe, "we should not consider that initiation always implies success in reaching the goal of its descent or its ascent" (43). There are no guarantees, and yet the alternative, stagnation in a status quo of endless competition and control, is unacceptable to many who have a sense that things could be better.

Sometimes, however, obstacles are misleading illusions; they can appear to be comfortable interludes or even "home" itself. As explained earlier, not all of Odysseus's obstacles were fearsome. His serene seven years on Calypso's isle were so peaceful that he was tempted to forget his quest and stay in the *wilderness*. Parsifal also had an opportunity to stop early in his adventures, at the Lady Blanchefor's castle. There he was considered the conquering hero, and could easily have succumbed to the subtle seduction of the known and comfortable. If he had accepted the invitations to stay and forsaken his impulse to proceed, he would never have encountered the Grail Castle. Likewise, many people are lulled into complacency by a lifestyle of relative ease and abundance. Even though we may not consider ourselves wealthy, by the standards of much of the rest of the world Americans are both greedy and wasteful, while enjoying relatively comfortable lives. When that status quo is challenged (say by higher gasoline prices, tariffs, limited access to consumer goods, or the exportation of jobs), rather than pursuing needed changes, many people become confused and defensive, victimized by their own Americentric delusions of grandeur and seduced by the known and the comfortable. They may seek to pin blame on their leaders, may "worship" the "golden idol" of consumerism as a salve for troubled minds (e.g., "when I feel stressed, I go shopping"), and may wander aimlessly for long periods of time accusing and attacking others on the planet for problems of their own making.

The Exodus. The Exodus provides a mythic example of an entire nation moving through the transition process on a grand scale. As Ray and Anderson suggest, "The Exodus is a wake-up tale of a cultural shift, a liberation manual about how people enslaved for generations can break a suffocating story line" (254). This story offers potentially valuable insights.

For Moses and the "children of Israel," the endings or separation occurred when they left Egypt _en masse._ Although they had experienced persecution as slaves to the Pharaoh, it took some convincing to get the people moving. Just as many organization members may be unhappy with the status quo but resist making changes, so too the Israelites chafed under bondage but many were reluctant to leave and step out into the wilderness. They had a clear "boundary marker:" the opening and subsequent closing of the Red Sea meant there was no going back. Likewise, creating boundary markers—even simple ones—can help both individuals and organizations acknowledge specific endings and move forward.

The Israelites spent forty years wandering in the wilderness on their way to the "Promised Land," so that ultimately, no one who left Egypt was alive to enter the new territory. It says in the Bible that along the way "the people murmured." As time wore on and they did not seem to be making sufficient progress toward their goal, people grew impatient, lost confidence in their leader, worshipped "false idols," and wistfully claimed their time under the Pharaoh had not been so bad after all. When the time finally came to realize their new beginnings in the "Promised Land," they had another literal threshold to mark the boundary between the wilderness and the new beginnings: the River Jordan. Lest they forget the journey they had completed in order to arrive at that crossing, they collected stones from the wilderness and carried them across the river to build an altar, which marked their gratitude and served as a symbol of remembrance.

Every element of this story is a metaphor for the process of making transitions in organizations and communities, and it provides a valuable teaching model for conveying the transition concept.

Key Actions for Organizational and Cultural Transitions

As an organizational development consultant, I am often called upon to provide "solutions," or at least perspectives, clues, and techniques to address complex workplace dilemmas. One of the most common situations I encounter is an organization stuck in old, binding traditions, while fully engaged in massive change and transition. In that instance, individual, organizational, and cultural transitions are often mirroring each other, and individuals are juggling changes and transitions at all levels simultaneously. All systems are in flux, and many people are responding either by retreating from the edge of change and clinging fiercely to tried and true traditions, or by looking to fix blame for the state of crisis, and plaintively calling for a "better patriarch." In that context, I have found there are **10 Key Actions** that are important in ensuring a successful transition:

- Allow for "Speaking the Unspeakable."
- Acknowledge endings and provide assistance for moving through the grief cycle.
- Recognize and support the process of working through the *wilderness*.
- Consciously involve people in managing transitions.
- Identify "early adopters," the "mainstream," and transition holdouts; then map a strategy for managing the transition with each group.
- Find ways to embrace those who do not fit "the mold," and teach people how to collaborate and build community.
- Preserve group memory and weave in new threads.
- Create rituals around transitional stages.
- Provide "time out" retreats.
- Celebrate success and prepare for the long haul.

(1) Allow for "Speaking the Unspeakable." Quite often those who raise difficult questions within an organizational milieu where that questioning translates into "speaking the unspeakable" are in turn the recipients of blame for organizational short-comings because to some it appears that they are bringing wounds into the open, much as Parsifal did when he directly questioned source of the Grail King's wound. The questioners become the criticized, as if they carry the onus of responsibility for "all the trouble around here," recalling Moses and his murmuring tribes. In the end, Parsifal brought healing by asking the crucial questions, and Moses brought deliverance by leading the reluctant tribes away from bondage. So, too, when the messenger is not "killed" or does not retreat into discouraged cynicism, those courageous agents of change can provide the impetus for critical organizational metamorphoses.

As discussed in chapter 3, many in positions of power try to control discourse at all costs, in order to avoid messy feelings that arise when the "walking wounded"—those who bear the shadow projections—start to talk about the "elephant in the middle of the room." The result all too often is that superficial treatments (mandatory trainings, employee counseling, shifting job roles and responsibilities, etc.) are reactively applied to so-called aberrant behavior. Managers seeking to show that their stopgap solutions appear to be working will point to a surface that appears relatively sound, yet may miss or ignore the infectious irritation that threatens both interpersonal relationships and organizational foundations.

(2) Acknowledge endings and provide assistance for moving through the grief cycle. Some declare that American culture itself is already in the midst of a transitional descent—one that fundamentalists believe can be only solved by "getting back to basics," or going back to the models of the past and perfecting the *power-over* system of control—while others contend a system-wide change is in order. Due to the massive changes and "endings" that have already occurred, Americans collectively are indeed already in the wilderness. To be sure, some endings have not been adequately acknowledged, thereby preventing those who have suffered losses an opportunity to grieve adequately, in order to resolve and let go of past injustices and move through their transition process. And, other than the vision articulated by Martin Luther King, Jr., no current or recent leader in the U.S. has articulated a clear and compelling vision of an alternate future that challenges Americentrism's reliance on patriarchal, *power-over* authority for deliverance.

Providing opportunities for individuals to tell their stories—to help them "feel heard" and move *through* the grief cycle (not getting stuck in the telling)—facilitates the resolution of their endings. For the very telling of stories alchemically translates the teller, just as Odysseus experienced when he told his tale to the Phaecians. The act of telling his story before a respectful audience produced a change in Odysseus' perspectives of himself, his adventures, and his place in the order of things. It provided a pivotal experience—a specific rite of passage in and of itself—that enabled him to proceed with his journey.

(3) Recognize and support the process of working through the *wilderness*. In the midst of massive changes, people may feel as if all moorings have been forcibly cut against their will and they are being set adrift. Any sense of integration and coherence in their lives has been destroyed as they have often been coerced to accept abrupt or alarming endings, and they find themselves in an unfamiliar, liminal, enigmatic, in-between place. They may feel as if competitive rivals, bureaucratic functionaries, or even well meaning friends and family have inflicted wounds in the process of leaving the old shores and attempting to navigate the wilderness. Thus, they often perceive attacks both by specific individuals and by an impersonal system upon which they suddenly realize they can no longer depend. In these situations, anger, betrayal, and other dysfunctional behavior are often pervasive throughout the organizational culture. Many employees are feeling stuck in the "neutral zone," or the *wilderness* descent, where nothing seems to make sense, it is difficult to regain traction for moving forward, threats abound in the shadows, and there is precious little light in the darkness.

The common impulse in this situation is often to work harder and faster: more of the same, usually with fewer resources. A few organizational leaders recognize the enormous return on their investment that can be garnered by recognizing the common challenges of the transition process and supporting their people through it. For example, Bridges experienced that some companies, like Intel, "put their people through enormous amounts of change and did so constantly" (*The Way of Transition* 148). Yet from his perspective, they were also cognizant of the inherent challenges and dangers, both for individual employees and for the organization. Although they did not devise a perfect or widespread solution, they at least initiated support by providing transition management training for all of the company's managers.

Although it would have been more helpful to provide transition sessions for all employees, the Intel investment paid important dividends. Bridges noticed, "Intel employees didn't talk about their *jobs* the way people did at other companies . . . they talked about their *assignments.*" This had the effect of "de-jobbing" the work processes, and virtually eliminating the old complaint (or excuse) of "that's not my job" (*Way of Transition* 149). In effect, by changing the identification of what was meant by a "job," the company introduced more flexibility and heightened the tolerance for ambiguity.

(4) Consciously involve people in managing transitions. Although the innovative Intel kind of approach to parceling out the work to be done was helpful in the transitions of a few companies, it remains the exception, rather than the norm. Bridges explains that in his experience, employees in other organizations who were having the rules changed around them often felt as if "they were being plunged headlong into a neutral zone that was frightening" and headed straight for disaster (151). That approach—imposing changes, along with imposing the company vision and values from *above*, rather than engaging participation in co-creating those elements—relies on motivation by fear, and is not conducive to sustaining long-term productivity and an effective workforce. In my experience, imposed changes often lead to compliance, without the enthusiasm and engagement of having been involved in their development. When employees do not have participation in the changes that affect them, apathy or resistance, whether overt or subtly covert, is often the result. On the other hand, when employees are engaged in identifying changes and in consciously managing transitions, as was the case with the NEFA, they have a sense of ownership in the process, which helps with handling the inherent difficulties of the passage.

(5) Identify "early adopters," the "mainstream," and transition holdouts; then map a strategy for managing the transition with each group. As those who are leading the progression through the transitional wilderness begin to approach the new beginnings, it is also important that they see what needs to be done to inform the mainstream workforce and to "bring up the rear." As Everett Rogers observes in his classic treatise *Diffusion of Innovations*, with any newly introduced innovation there will always be some "early adopters" who will quickly recognize the benefits of proposed changes. They are also ready and willing to experiment with its creation and act as "change agents." Of course, there will also be the majority of the workforce or the community who will be simply doing their work or leading their lives, largely unaware of the proposal or even the need for dramatic changes. Finally, there will be a minority who will stridently resist the changes, either because they resist change *per se* or because they have vested interests in maintaining the status quo.

Forty years of research on the implementation and diffusion of innovations has shown that efforts to move a group to accept changes are best spent with the large majority in the middle. It is also important to enlist simultaneously both the assistance of enthusiastic early adopters and change agents, and work to reveal the vested interests of the reactionary group, or those who are resisting the change at all costs. In my experience, those who have profited from the status quo are unlikely to "see the light" and willingly surrender their vested interests. Nevertheless, this situation serves to reinforce the dictum that the most important thing that can be done in moving through transition is to provide honest communication about what is happening and what to expect. The challenge for the facilitator is to help the group move into the space of greater ambiguity in which vested interests and past assumptions can be unpacked, and where they often reveal their failing utility. During this stage, it is especially critical that communication occurs more often than has been previously thought necessary, and through as many different channels as can be accessed.

(6) Find ways to embrace those who do not fit "the mold," and teach people how to collaborate and build community. There is a deep wound that has never been completely healed and is festering in American culture at large, a wound that diminishes our abilities to cope effectively with the upheaval of these times and that inhibits our transition. This is the wound created as a result of centuries of highly structured, dualistic thinking and dogma that occurs when individuals who do not fit the Americentric cultural *mold* are labeled, denigrated, stifled, excluded, and ultimately *othered.* Those who have suffered from the wounding of any variation of *rankism* are often left with a disability that may be difficult to understand for those who have enjoyed inherent—and often invisible—privilege and therefore are not similarly afflicted. In the interest of moving on, they are tempted to impatiently suggest, "Get over it!" (Fuller).

This wound operates covertly in U.S. organizations and the culture at large, where it impedes productive responses to massive systemic changes, while clues to the wound's depth and seriousness are ignored and avoided. This dynamic is an organizational mirroring of the families who impose an implicit rule that no one will talk about an adult child who failed to live the unimaginative role imposed by the father, thereby challenging his patriarchal control. Likewise, in the organizational context, individuals' contributions and ideas may be dismissed because they are not in the inner circle, or they may not adequately fit the company mold or speak the language of the establishment and are therefore not accepted or "blessed" by the patriarchs.

Rather than invest in dialogue or community building methods, many organizations avoid the time-intensive and often confusing processes involved in developing true consensus and collaboration, and write them off as "not pragmatic" and "too touchy-feely." They settle for command-and-control management and for "groupthink;" thus they do not take fuller advantage of broader skills and diverse perspectives inherent in the workforce. Yet, these same command-and-control patriarchs will wonder aloud why they are having internal strife, lower productivity, and reduced efficiency; rather than seek deeper systemic change, they get busy looking for someone to blame.

In the transitional wilderness stage, organizational members who may have clearly seen and initially agreed with the need for change will often throw up their hands in resignation and declare, "It's not working. We will have to go back to the structure we had." There is often wistful talk of the "good old days." Bridges explains why transitions will often bring old turf battles or dysfunctional relationships to the surface: "Transition is like the low-pressure area on the organizational weather map. It attracts all the storms and conflicts in the area, past and present" (*Organizations in Transition* 3). Yet there is also opportunity in this storminess, because by bringing lingering conflicts to the surface, they have conscious awareness and the possibility to be healed. Indeed, in my experience, true progress cannot be made until these conflicts have received more than token attention and been adequately addressed.

(7) Preserve group memory and weave in new threads. Preservation of the group or organizational memory is especially critical, not as a place to return to, but as a foundation to build upon. It is important that the preserved memory does not just focus on "the good old days," rather it carries the reasons the changes and transitions are necessary. Senge suggests that the mental models that are the repository of an organization's collective history provide an important context for meaningful change and transition. Working with those models (or myths) offers an effective way to cope consciously and creatively with transitions (174), in that acknowledging and honoring individual and organizational memories is an important part of the process of letting go and moving on.

Collective memory is only a thread, a part of the whole, not the goal. Having the known, dependable threads of the past pulled out and our vulnerability exposed—as individuals, within organizations, or as a nation—is excruciating for many. Nevertheless, new *kairos* openings provide hopeful opportunities for creative new patterns. The key to surviving the organization's transitional wilderness period lies in loosely weaving the threads of collective memory, of shared (not imposed) vision, of consciously chosen and agreed upon group norms, of conscious team and/or community building, and of newly integrated understanding and growth. This is the weave that can help sustain organizational travelers through Odyssean whirlpools, encounters with monsters, and descents into the underworld that may be required as they traverse their own transformational wilderness.

(8) Create rituals around transitional stages. Providing both an understanding of initiations and transitions and a "ritual container" for making the journey can both help shape deep level changes and develop trust. Rather than some esoteric practice, as many Americans fear, ritual is the practice of marking an occasion, event, or transition in some symbolic way. Starhawk explains, "Rituals create a group bond. They help build community." They can be simple or complex, and they help to create a container within which the transition process can be completed. Furthermore, Starhawk observes, "Rituals are part of every culture. They are the events that bind a culture together, that create a heart, a center for the people" (*Dreaming the Dark* 155). The concept of creating rituals is not to be taken lightly. Mythologist Michael Meade describes ritual as the creation of "crucibles" for the fires of change: "Without a ritual to contain and inform the wounds of life, pain and suffering increase, yet meaningful change doesn't occur" (*"Rites of Passage"*30). If the change does not fully occur, then we are doomed to repeat the mistakes of the past. In that light, the rituals of ancient wisdom cultures have much to offer for twenty-first century transitional journeys.

(9) Provide "time out" retreats. One of the most valuable methods of coping with the challenges of transition and transformation requires reframing the concept of *wilderness*. Rather than solely defining the *wilderness* period as a liminal time of chaos and confusion, or even as an initiatory descent, *wilderness* can be held as a place one can purposefully visit for healing respite. In that vein, ancient wisdom traditions create intentional transitional spaces apart—whether a vision quest, the ceremonial kiva, or the women's "red tent"—that provide an opportunity for a temporary withdrawal from outer actions in order to assist people in making the passage into a new way of being.

This concept of leaving home or the regular workspace and intentionally entering into a liminal space—whether for a spiritual cleansing or rebirth, or to examine carefully the threads of one's transition—is gaining favor in American culture. Individuals embark on retreats that require extended "time out" from the speed of their daily routine. Organizational groups leave the office for retreats that range from basic teambuilding to creating deep soulful connections, which foster trust and a sense of community. Even the United States Navy is now providing a transitional session for warriors returning home from deployment, in order to help them psychologically make the shift from their wartime persona to that of parent and/or partner. The underlying formidable task, for a culture predicated on systematic organization and tight control, is to reframe the liminal space. Rather than avoiding its chaos and confusion, it can be held as a time and space away from the daily routine to examine carefully the sources of upheaval. Then, if need be, steps can be taken to heal the involved relationships and to provide the support needed for the emergence of new understandings and collaborative alliances.

(10) Celebrate success and prepare for the long haul. There is a certain camaraderie that develops when people have made a difficult passage together in a way that promotes interdependence and partnership, rather than competition. If they have allowed themselves to be open to sharing their difficulties and fears, and encouraged to ask for help from their fellow travelers rather than expecting or attempting to heroically go it alone, a trust develops and endures through many difficult and formidable tasks. In the case of consciously managing transitions as a partnership, the group has also developed its own operating system for navigating future transitions. This work builds a sense of confidence that group members will not be destroyed by the winds of change, and that they can rely on their co-workers when the going gets tough, and that accomplishment deserves to be celebrated. Honor both individual and collective contributions, and call attention to the hard work, perseverance, and effective collaborations that have occurred, and offer public praise and recognition.

It is also important to help people understand that there will always be transitions to be navigated in our lives. This is not a matter of sticking it out or even managing until things go "back to normal." Philosopher and Jungian analyst Helene Shulman (Lorenz) notes in *Living at the Edge of Chaos*, "Healing work involves forming and reforming our models of the world and our praxis in ever new rituals of integration . . . that can never be done once and for all" (238). Thus, those who would be the facilitators and maieutic mentors of a new cultural model need to sign up for the long haul. Starhawk explains, "Transforming culture is a long-term project . . . but though power-from-within can burst forth in an instant, its rising is mostly a process slow as the turning wheels of generations" (*Dreaming the Dark* 180). In order to reach the "tipping point," there is much groundwork to be completed and many setbacks to be endured. This process will take time and patience; there is not a moment to spare.

Emergent Patterns: Networks by Design

When spider webs unite, they can stop a lion.
&Ancient Ethiopian Proverb

Whether meeting in circles, building community, coalescing around a common cause, or working to incorporate a sense of "team-ness" in the workplace, there are emerging networks of people committed to making a difference in many American neighborhoods and organizations. Most likely, a few seed individuals in each instance are promoting gatherings and "calling the circle." They are the individuals reporter Malcom Gladwell refers to in *The Tipping Point* as *connectors*, who together with the information gatherers, or *mavens*, and the *salesmen* who persuade others to become engaged in trends and social action, are building a large-scale movement, or "social epidemic." Gladwell notes, "The success of any kind of social epidemic is heavily dependent on the involvement of people with a particular and rare set of gifts" (33). Foremost, they hear the call, and then are willing to answer that call and become engaged.

The spark of hope for developing collaborative models of interacting, governing, and doing business is kindled in those who recognize the need to make serious, far-reaching changes in the cultural fabric. In Diffusion Theory terms, they are the *innovators*, who may not be parts of the organizational or cultural mainstream, yet they are able to design new approaches uniquely tailored to a particular situation. They must articulate them in such a way that the *early adopters* and *change agents* within the organization, community, or constituency can grasp their importance and make practical applications. Perhaps they already feel somewhat liminal within this culture, yet they are willing to answer the call to help things change.

These liminal individuals might be Returned Peace Corps Volunteers who came home from their service abroad with "new eyes," and never really "fit in" to the mainstream culture. They might be immigrants seeking to manage the tricky balance between retaining their cultural roots and adapting to new mores and policies. They might even be natives who, for a variety of reasons, feel like immigrants in their own land. As Mary Catherine Bateson recalls in *Full Circles, Overlapping Lives*, "I have learned to work on the assumption that my daughter and I were born in different countries, not according to our passports but because our country has changed, making me an immigrant from the past" (4). These "liminal beings" might also be children raised in multicultural homes, unsure of where they belong. They might come from the ranks of the "walking wounded" among us who carry the shadow trauma of inexplicable horrors. Or perhaps they will be those who have somehow glimpsed the promise of wholeness and freedom, never again to be content with the fragmented, competitive status quo.

Separately, these individuals may feel as if their efforts make very little difference. Yet, collectively, they contribute to the rising tide of an increasingly networked movement that is calling for true democracy, social justice, and partnership with the earth. Even when confronting huge corporate interests that are bent on plundering our heritage, their efforts—however small—do matter, as they add up to create the "tipping point" (Gladwell). As Robert F. Kennedy pronounced in a speech given in South Africa in 1966:

> It is from numberless diverse acts of courage and belief that human history is shaped. Each time a person stands up for an idea, or acts to improve the lot of others, or strikes out against injustice, he [or she] sends forth a tiny ripple of hope, and crossing each other from a million different centers of energy and daring, those ripples build a current that can sweep down the mightiest walls of oppression and resistance.

Indeed, those disparate individual actions can have long-term importance, and together, these partnership builders make an enormous difference; they create global synergy where the cumulative effects of their individual efforts are truly greater than the simple sum of the individual parts. As soul psychologists Craig Schindler and Gary Lapid, in *The Great Turning* contend, while "the Great Turning begins with the individual," it proceeds to "the legacy we will leave our children" (141). Thus, we each are being called to spin our connecting webs by fostering understanding, designing new patterns, and creating networks, as partners in transformation.

Conclusions: Weaving the Web

Fortunately, in the face of the outrage and despair generated by a patriarchal, *power-over* system that appears to have a stranglehold on the minds, media, money, and manipulative power of American society, threads of hope are appearing throughout that self-same society. While achieving a partnership society is by no means a foregone conclusion, there is an enormous — though currently largely unseen — potential for its realization. Bateson observes, "All of us live today at a crossroads where the most ancient of human paths converge." Contrary to the fragmentation and "othering" of a system bent on domination and control, she suggests, "In this time of accelerating convergence we have access to a greater range of what it means to be human than ever before, but the willingness to learn and to be changed is fragile and vulnerable to fatigue and fear" (17). Calling forth the energy and resources of the *Cultural Creatives*, the wisdom of initiated elders, and the invaluable spark of intrepid young people, we can, in the words of the *Gather the Women* organizers, "hospice the old paradigm while midwifing the new."

Midwifing connotes bringing out a new being from within, and recognizing that that "being" may not have been one's own conception, although as members of organizations and communities there are opportunities to co-create innovative solutions to complex dilemmas, and assist in the safe and healthy delivery of the outcomes. "Giving birth" in Spanish is "dar la luz," or "bring to the light; to give new sight." Likewise, while demonstrations and holding actions, creation of alternate structures, and concerted counteractive media campaigns all have a cumulative, important effect, surface actions alone will not suffice for this massive sea change that involves a whole new way of seeing things. Conventional wisdom holds that this change will not come quickly. As La Chappelle acknowledges, "It is not easy to bring into the world a new way of seeing, of acting, of living. An internal struggle takes place every day between old patterns of response and new patterns of soulful living" (160).

Those new patterns await discovery with the asking of the Parsifalian question: *"What ails thee?"* What ails our families, our workplaces, our society, and our world? Where can we make small changes in our responses and larger changes in the way we organize ourselves and consciously form our webs of connection? How can we unleash the collaborative power of partnerships and generate the greening of the wasteland around the mythical Grail Castle?

Psychotherapist Robert Sardello suggests, "The Grail is the soul of the world," or the *anima mundi* (12). At a time when the popularity of *The Da Vinci Code* has refocused attention on the Grail myth, this is particularly opportune. He continues, "The renewal of the world does not consist in the finding of the Grail . . . This story informs us that the point of seeking the soul of the world is in the seeking, in paying attention to what is abandoned" (20). It appears that what has been abandoned, or sacrificed in the American society entrenched in a *power-over* system of competition and control is not only the fragile ones—the children, the endangered species, the water, and the air—but also the consciousness that Sardello concludes has itself become "diseased" (30). Consequently, the land around the Grail Castle has become a wasteland of shopping malls and corporate platitudes, where we are not even sure today's young heroes are seeking the healing Grail.

Once again, myth points out a passageway through the difficulties of our times. As Jean Houston claims, "We look to creator myths to discover what to do to re-create our world—and most important, what not to do to raise up monsters and aberrations" (*The Hero and the Goddess* 375). Just as heroism represents the mythic tap root for American society, so too heroic organizations are needed that will answer the call to courageously move away from the status quo, or "business as usual," and enter relatively uncharted territory. In order to move beyond the paralysis instituted by *power-over* systems, the world also needs mediators and bridge builders of communication; between cultures and the great religions and faith traditions of the world, between men and women, and between competing interests in our own organizations and communities. Houston contends that we are called to be "conduits for a new order of reality," and that in fact, "we are direct participants in the story of the *anima mundi* . . . the Soul in the World" (376). Those who choose to participate in the building are also challenged to be weavers: to bring together myriad threads into new patterns, while carefully holding the tension and simultaneously keeping a finger on the *zeitgeist* pulse.

The building has already begun. "Somewhere out there in the world," writes mythologist Maggie Macary, "which has now become woven into an inter-net (sic), people meet and share dreams and visions, stories and poems, experiencing the translucent nature of symbols" (*Arrows*

6/30/03). Within this web, as the *Cultural Creatives* gather around various causes, there are numerous "portals" into an ever-widening array of websites that reflect their concerns. As MoveOn.org and VoteNoWar.org have demonstrated by quickly generating large donations and huge numbers of protestors, the Internet offers an enormous capacity to catalyze massive groups of people in very short periods of time.

The transition beyond the patriarchal system of *power-over* and into *power-with* partnerships will not occur easily. Those who have vested interests in maintaining the status quo have too much to lose in allowing changes to take place. Nevertheless, there is a growing company of individuals who are committed to weaving the fabric of a new culture. There are the creative innovators, the courageous change agents and early adopters, and the dedicated transformers who have recognized the vision, and heard the call to move beyond self-interest and consider the common good. The have taken up the challenge to realize the vision of changing the story. Those who are committed to this path need inspiration, information, and skills for the arduous journey ahead. They also need partners, for no one is asked nor needs to travel alone.

Caminante, no hay camino.
Se hace camino al andar.

(Traveler, there is no road.
You make the road by walking.)

&. Antonio Machado

✎ Glossary ✍

Myth: A story held by an individual or a group of people that describes where they have been, who they are, where they are going, and the meanings of the mysteries in their lives. Mythic stories are often comprised of symbols, metaphors, and examples that portray the underlying meaning, values, and norms for that group.

Organization: Any grouping of individuals that shares a common purpose and structure. This may be in reference to work/economic systems, social/community systems, political systems, or educational systems.

Partnership: A social system of inclusion based on networks of shared responsibility for agenda-setting, decision-making, and project outcomes, which rely on commitment to open communication, mutual respect, individual dignity, equal opportunity, power sharing, and servant leadership.

Patriarchy: An institutionalized social *system* that depends on top-down hierarchies of exclusion, domination, and control, which are based on power differences where one person (or a small group) is vested with varying degrees of control over everyone else in the household, the organization, or the nation.

Power-over: Control achieved through dominance relationships based on unequal power.

Power-with: Shared control wherein everyone has the opportunity to collaborate and affect one's own life while also considering the common good.

❧ Bibliography ❧

Abdullah, Sharif. *Creating a World That Works for All.* San Francisco: Berrett-Koehler, 1999.

Anzaldúa, Gloria. *Borderlands/La Frontera: The New Mestiza.* San Francisco: Aunt Lute, 1999.

Armas, Genaro C. "Survey: 1.4 million more live in poverty." *Santa Barbara News-Press,* 3 September 2003, B-1.

Arrien, Angeles. *Signs of Life: The Five Universal Shapes and How to Use Them.* Sonoma: Arcus, 1992.

Autry, James A., and Stephen Mitchell. "Beyond Machiavelli: The Source of Real Power." *Utne Reader* (Sept.-Oct. 1998): 85-87.

Baldwin, Christina. *Calling the Circle: The First and Future Culture.* Newberg, OR: Swan-Raven, 1994.

Bateson, Mary Catherine. *Composing a Life.* New York: Plume, 1989.

---. *Full Circles, Overlapping Lives: Culture and Generation in Transition.* New York: Ballantine, 2000.

Belenky, Mary Field, Blythe McVicker Clinchy, Nancy Rule Goldberger, & Jill Mattuck Tarule. *Women's Ways of Knowing: The Development of Self, Voice and Mind.* New York: Basic, 1986.

Bell, Yvonne, Cathy L. Bouie, & Joseph A. Baldwin. "Afrocentric Cultural Consciousness and African

American Male-Female Relationships." *Afrocentric Visions: Studies in Culture and Communication*. Ed. Janice D. Hamlet. Thousand Oaks, CA: Sage, 1998, 47-71.

Bennett, J. "Transition Shock: Putting culture shock in perspective." *International and Intercultural Communication Annual* (4) 1977: 45-52.

Bennis, Warren, & Bert Namus, *Leaders: Strategies for Taking Charge,* 2nd Edition. New York: HarperBusiness, 2003.

Block, Peter. *Stewardship: Choosing Service Over Self-Interest.* San Francisco: Berrett-Koehler, 1993.

Boggs, Grace. "Journey to New America." *Yes!* Fall 2002:58-59.

Bolen, Jean Shinoda. *Goddesses in Older Women: Archetypes in Women Over Fifty.* New York: HarperCollins, 2001.

---. *The Millionth Circle: How to Change Ourselves and the World.* Berkeley: Conari, 1999.

Bridges, William. *Managing Transitions.* Reading, MA: Addison-Wesley, 1990.

---. *The Way of Transition: Embracing Life's Most Difficult Moments.* Cambridge, MA: Perseus, 2001.

Brown, Joseph Epes. *The Spiritual Legacy of the American Indian.* New York: Crossroads, 1982.

Buber, Martin. *The Knowledge of Man: A Philosophy of the Interhuman.* New York: Harper & Row, 1966.

Cockburn, Cynthia. *In the Way of Women: Men's Resistance to Sex Equality in Organizations.* Ithaca: ILR, 1991.

Cousineau, Phil. *Once and Future Myths: The Power of Ancient Stories in Modern Times.* Berkeley: Conari, 2001.

Eck, Diana L., *A New Religious America: How a "Christian Country" Has Become the World's Most Religiously Diverse Nation.* San Francisco: HarperSanFrancisco, 2001.

Eire, Carlos. "Digging at the roots of Christian intolerance." *Los Angeles Times Book Review,* 10 August 2003, R-4.

Eisler, Riane. *The Chalice & the Blade: Our History, Our Future.* San Francisco: Harper, 1987.

---. *The Power of Partnership: Seven Relationships that Will Change Your Life.* Novato, CA: New World, 2002.

---. and David Loye. *The Partnership Way: New Tools for Living and Learning. Healing Our Families, Our Communities, and Our World.* San Francisco: Harper, 1990.

---. and Alfonso Montuori. "The Partnership Organization: A Systems Approach." *OD Practitioner*, 33.2 (2001). Online posting. www.partnershipway.org/html/subpages/articles/organization.htm

Eller, Cynthia. *The Myth of Matriarchal Prehistory: Why an Invented Past Won't Give Women a Future.* Boston: Beacon, 2000.

Emery, Merrelyn, ed. *Participative Design for Participative Democracy.* Canberra, Australia: Australian National U, 1993.

Fisher, Roger and William Ury. *Getting to Yes: Negotiating Agreement Without Giving In, 2nd Edition.* New York: Penguin, 1991.

Flinders, Carol Lee. *At the Root of This Longing: Reconciling a Spiritual Hunger and a Feminist Thirst.* San Francisco: Harper, 1998.

---. *Rebalancing the World: Why Women Belong and Men Compete and How to Restore the Ancient Equilibrium.* San Francisco: Harper, 2002.

Fortunoff, David. "Dialogue, Dialectic, and Maieutic: Plato's Dialogues as Educational Models." Online posting. 20 November 2003. www.bu.edu/wcp/Papers/Anci/Ancifort.html

Freire, Paulo. *Pedagogy of the Oppressed.* New York: Continuum, 2000.

French, Marilyn. *Beyond Power: On Men, Women, and Morals.* New York: Summit, 1985.

Fuller, Robert W. *Sombodies and Nobodies: Overcoming the Abuse of Rank.* Gabriola Island, BC: New Society, 2003.

Gannon, Martin J. *Understanding Global Cultures: Metaphorical journeys through 23 nations.* Thousand Oaks, CA: Sage, 2001.

Gauthier, Alain. "The Challenge of Stewardship: Building Learning Organizations in Healthcare." *Learning Organizations: Developing Cultures for Tomorrow's Workplace.* Ed. Sarita Chawla and John Renesch. Portland: Productivity P, 1995.

Giegerich, Wolfgang. *The Soul's Logical Life.* New York: Peter Lang, 1998.

Gladwell, Malcolm. *The Tipping Point: How Little Things Can Make a Big Difference.* New York: Little, Brown, and Company, 2000.

Golden, Stephanie. *Slaying the Mermaid: Women and the Culture of Sacrifice.* New York: Three Rivers P, 1998.

Goleman, Daniel. *Emotional Intelligence: Why it can matter more than IQ.* New York: Bantam, 1995.

Greene, Robert, and Joost Elffers. "The Laws of Power." *Utne Reader* (Sept.-Oct. 1998): 78-84.

Greenleaf, Robert. "Servant Leadership." Online. 17 November 2003. www.greenleaf.org.

Guggenbühl, Allan. *Men, Power, and Myths: The Quest for Male Identity.* New York: Continuum, 1997.

Guinier, Lani. *The Tyranny of the Majority: Fundamental Fairness in a Representative Democracy*. New York: Free P, 1994.

Hawkins, David R. *Power vs Force: The Hidden Determinants of Human Behavior*. Carlsbad, CA: Hay House, 2002.

Helgeson, Sally. *The Female Advantage: Women's Ways of Leadership*. New York: Doubleday Currency, 1990.

Henderson, Joseph, and Maud Oakes. *The Wisdom of the Serpent: The Myths of Death, Rebirth, and Resurrection*. Princeton: Princeton UP, 1963.

Hillman, James. *Kinds of Power: A Guide to its Intelligent Uses*. New York: Doubleday, 1995.

---. *The Soul's Code: In Search of Character and Calling*. New York: Warner, 1996.

Hock, Dee. *Birth of the Chaordic Age*. San Francisco: Berrett-Koehler, 1999.

Hollis, James. *Tracking the Gods: The Place of Myth in Modern Life*. Toronto: Inner City, 1995.

Houston, Jean. *The Hero and the Goddess: The Odyssey as Mystery and Initiation*. New York: Ballantine, 1992.

---. *Jump Time: Shaping Your Future in a World of Radical Change*. New York: Tarcher/Putnam, 2000.

---. *Manual for the Peacemaker: An Iroquois Legend to Heal Self and Society*. Wheaton, IL: Quest, 1995.

Hubbard, Barbara Marx. *Conscious Evolution: Awakening the Power of Our Social Potential.* New York: New World Library, 1998.

Iogna-Prat, Dominique. *Order and Exclusion: Cluny and Christendom Face Heresy, Judaism, and Islam (1000-1150).* Ithaca: Cornell UP, 2003.

Isaacs, William. "Dialogue," *The Fifth Discipline Fieldbook: Strategies and Tools for Building a Learning Organization,* Senge, Peter, Charlotte Roberts, Richard B. Ross, Bryan J. Smith, and Art Kleiner. New York: Currency, 1994.

James, Frank. "More in U.S. living in poverty." *Santa Barbara News-Press,* 27 September 2003, B-1.

Johnson, Allan G. *The Gender Knot: Unraveling our Patriarchal Legacy.* Philadelphia: Temple UP, 1997.

---. *Privilege, Power, and Difference.* Mountain View, CA: Mayfield, 2001.

Johnson, Robert A. *Feminity Lost and Regained.* New York: Harper & Row, 1990.

---. *He: Understanding Masculine Psychology.* New York: Harper & Row, 1990.

Kalven, Janet. "Respectable Outlaw." *Bread Not Stones.* Citation by Elisabeth Schüssler-Fiorenza. Boston: Beacon, 1984, dedication.

Kim, Young Yun. "Intercultural Adaptation," *Handbook of International and Intercultural Communication.* Eds. Molefi Kete Asanta and William Gudykunst. Newbury Park, CA: Sage, 1989. 275-294.

La Chapelle, David. *Navigating the Tides of Change: Stories from Science, the Sacred, and a Wise Planet.* Gabriola Island, BC: New Society, 2001.

Lavoie, Denise. "Probe: Church abused 1,000." *Santa Barbara News-Press,* 24 July 2003, B-1.

Lerner, Gerda. *The Creation of Patriarchy.* New York: Oxford UP, 1986.

Lincoln, Bruce. *Emerging from the Chrysalis: Rituals of Women's Initiation.* New York: Oxford UP, 1991.

Macary, Maggie. *Arrows.* Online. 30 June 2003. www.mythandculture.com.

Macy, Joanna and Molly Young Brown. *Coming Back to Life: Practices to Reconnect Our Lives, Our World.* Gabriola Island, BC: New Society, 1998.

Mahdi, Louise Carus, Steven Foster, & Meredith Little (Eds.). *Betwixt and Between: Patterns of Masculine and Feminine Initiation.* La Salle, IL: Open Court, 1987.

Meade, Michael. "Rites of Passage at the End of the Millenium." *Crossroads: The Quest for Contemporary Rites of Passage.* Eds. Louise Carus Mahdi, Nancy Geyer Christopher, and Michael Meade. Chicago: Open Court, 1996. 27-33.

Monick, Eugene. *Phallos: Sacred Image of the Masculine.* Toronto: Inner City, 1987.

Naranjo, Claudio. *The End of Patriarchy: And the Dawning of the Tri-une Society.* Oakland, CA: Amber Lotus, 1994.

Ochs, Carol. *Behind the Sex of God: Toward a New Consciousness—Transcending Matriarchy and Patriarchy.* Boston: Beacon, 1978.

Peck, M. Scott. *The Road Less Traveled: A New Psychology of Love, Traditional Values and Spiritual Growth.* New York: Simon & Schuster, 1978.

Pennington, Dorothy L. "Interpersonal Power and Influence in Intercultural Communication." *Handbook of International and Intercultural Communication.* Ed. Molefi Kete Asante and William Gudykunst. Newbury Park: Sage, 1989.

Pike, Diane Kennedy. "The New Paradigm of Partnership." *Gather the Women Page.* Online. 30 November 2003. www.gatherthewomen.org/creations/pike.html

Porter, W. Marc, and Isaac E. Catt. "The Narcissistic Reflection of Communicative Power: Delusions of Progress Against Organizational Discrimination." *Narrative and Social Control: Critical Perspectives.* Ed. Dennis K. Mumby. Newbury Park: Sage, 1993. 164-85.

Ray, Paul H., and Sherry Ruth Anderson. *The Cultural Creatives: How 50 Million People are Changing the World.* New York: Harmony, 2000.

Robinson, John C. *Death of a Hero, Birth of the Soul: Answering the Call of Midlife*. Tulsa, OK: Council Oak, 1995.

Rogers, Everett. *Diffusion of Innovations, Third Edition*. New York: Free P, 1983.

Sardello, Robert. *Facing the World with Soul: The Reimagination of Modern Life*. Hudson, NY: Lindisfarne, 1992.

Schachter-Shalomi, Zalman, and Ronald S. Miller. *From Age-ing to Sage-ing: A Profound New Vision of Growing Older*. New York: Warner, 1995.

Schindler, Craig, and Gary Lapid. *The Great Turning*. Santa Fe: Bear & Company, 1989.

---., and Cynthia King. "Hope Out of the Ashes: Being a Light in the Darkness." Workshop, Leadership Improvement Training (LIT) Conference, San Diego, CA, 2003.

---., and Cynthia King. "The Soul of Leadership: Being a Light in Dark Times." Workshop, Leadership Improvement Training (LIT) Conference, San Diego, CA, 1999.

Seidler, Victor Jeleniewski. "Men, power, control and violence." *Working with men for change*. Ed. Jim Wild. London: UCL P, 1999. 181-96.

Senge, Peter M. *The Fifth Discipline: The Art and Practice of the Learning Organization*. New York: Doubleday, 1990.

Shephard, Molly, www.womenof.com

Shulman, Helene. *Living at the Edge of Chaos: Complex Systems in Culture and Psyche*. Einsiedeln: Daimon, 1997.

Somé, Malidoma Patrice. *The Healing Wisdom of Africa: Finding Life Purpose Through Nature, Ritual, and Community*. New York: Jeremy Tarcher/Putnam, 1998.

Starhawk. *Dreaming the Dark: Magic, Sex and Politics*. Boston: Beacon, 1997.

---. *Webs of Power: Notes From the Global Uprising*. Gabriola Island, BC: New Society, 2002.

Stein, Murray and John Hollwitz, Eds. *Psyche at Work: Workplace Applications of Jungian Analytical Psychology*. Wilmette, IL: Chiron,1995.

Stone, Sidra. *The Shadow King: The Invisible Force That Holds Women Back*. Mill Valley, CA: Nataraj, 1997.

Tarnas, Richard. *The Passion of the Western Mind: Understanding the Ideas That Have Shaped Our World View*. New York: Ballantine, 1991.

---. "Is the modern psyche undergoing a rite of passage?" *The Vision Thing: Myth, Politics and Psyche in the World*. Thomas Singer, Ed. New York: Routledge, 2000.

Turner, Victor. *The Ritual Process*. Chicago: Aldine, 1969.

Van Gennep, Arnold. *The Rites of Passage*. Trans. Monika
B. Vizedom and Gabrielle L. Caffee. Chicago: U of
Chicago P, 1960.

Wagner, Sally Roesch. *Sisters in Spirit: Haudenosaunee
(Iroquois) Influence on Early American Feminists*.
Summertown: Native Voices, 2001.

Wall, Steve. *Wisdom's Daughters: Conversations with
Women Elders of Native America*. New York:
HarperCollins, 1993.

Wheatley, Margaret J. *Finding Our Way: Leadership For an
Uncertain Time*. San Francisco: Berrett-Koehler,
2005.

---. *Leadership and the New Science: Discovering Order in a
Chaotic World*. San Francisco: Berrett-Koehler,
1999.

---. "The Promise and Paradox of Community." *Margaret
Wheatley Page*. 29 October 2003.
www.margaretwheatley.com.

Woodman, Marion. *The Ravaged Bridegroom: Masculinity
in Women*. Toronto: Inner City, 1990.

❦ Index ❧

A

Abdullah, Sharif, 2
Addictions, 10, 73, 188
American Woodmark, 129
Americentrism, 2, 11, 32, 64, 72, 155, 166, 191, 194, 198
Anderson, Sherry Ruth, 35-6, 48, 163, 171, 173-4, 177-8,
      182, 189, 191
Annenberg Public Policy Center, 25
Anzaldúa, Gloria, 175
Armas, Genaro, 9
Arrien, Angeles, 163
Athena, 4, 122
Autry, James, 107

B

Baldwin, Cristina, 105-6, 162-3, 172
Bateson, Mary Catherine, 44, 205-6
Baxter International, 129
Belenky, Mary Field, 57, 60
Bennett, J., 190
Bennis, Warren, 99
Blanchard, Ken, 99
Block, Peter, 28, 66, 116-9, 136
Boggs, Grace Lee, 4
Bolen, Jean Shinoda, 163, 166
Bonaparte, Napoleon, 73
Bridge, The/IFLAC, 131
Bridges, William, 136, 178-81, 185-8, 196, 199-200
Brown, Joseph Epes, 158
Brown, Molly Young, 78
Buber, Martin, 165

C
Catt, Isaac, 70
Center for International Dialogue, 65
Chaordic Commons, 129
Chiang, Pamela, 4
Cockburn, Cynthia, 14, 23-4, 74, 77, 105
Columbus, Christopher, 72
Common Ground Model, 83-98
Consensus, 53
Cook, Melissa, 109
Cousineau, Phil, 122-4
Cultural Creatives, 35-6, 49, 81, 174, 182, 206, 209
Culture shock, 190

D
Deganawidah, 159-60
Democracy, 5, 159, 205
Dialogue, 164-5
Diffusion Theory, 166, 197, 204
Diversity training, 55-6
Domestication, 67
Dupont, 129

E
Eck, Diana, 154
Einstein, Albert, 65, 170
Eire, Carlos, 19
Eisler, Riane, 17, 21-2, 39-40, 42, 48-52, 54, 56, 128
Elffers, Joost, 68
Eller, Cynthia, 109
Emery, Merrelyn, 110, 136
Eradication, 67
Eurocentrism, 2, 11, 32

Shephard, Molly, 25
Shulman, Helene, 203
Situational Leadership, 99
Smith, John, 157-8
Somé, Malidoma Patrice, 156, 158
Starhawk, 67, 70, 73, 76-9, 81, 115, 153, 201, 203
Steelcase, 130
Stein, Murray, 20
Stone, Sidra, 34

T
Tarnas, Richard, 20
Taylor, Shelley, 17
Team front, 29
Tipping point, 166, 204-5
Tomlin, Lily, 8
Total Quality Management (TQM), 30
Turner, Victor, 177-8

U
Ury, William, 137

V
Van Gennep, Arnold, 177-8
Vernon, Rama, 65
VISA, 129
Volvo, 128

W
Wagner, Sally, 159
Wall, Steve, 160
Web, 67, 155
Wheatley, Margaret, 48, 102, 116, 119, 156, 161-2, 174, 179
Women of Vision and Action (WOVA), 65
Woodman, Marion, 34

Sometimes we feel too small to make a difference, in the face of such enormous organizational and global challenges. It is important to remember that we are not alone; there are potential partners also seeking a sense of community. It is also important to recognize that no matter how small or insignificant our gifts may seem, our actions do make a difference. Consider these wise words by the poet Bonaro Overstreet:

STUBBORN OUNCES
(To One Who Doubts the Worth of Doing Anything
if You Can't Do Everything)

You say the little efforts that I make
Will do no good; they will never prevail
To tip the hovering scale
Where justice hangs in the balance.
                    I don't think
I ever thought they would.
But I am prejudiced beyond debate
In favor of my right to choose which side
Shall feel the stubborn ounces of my weight.

❧ Acknowledgements ❧

I have stood upon the shoulders of giants and been inspired and helped by a company of angels and champions in the writing of this book; it truly represents a partnership effort.

I have studied and been sourced by the writings and speeches of many deeply insightful and visionary guides. They include Margaret Wheatley, Starhawk, Allan Johnson, Jean Houston, Angeles Arrien, Riane Eisler, Barbara Marx Hubbard, Dame Anita Roddick, Cristina Baldwin, William Bridges, Carol Lee Flinders, Elisabet Sahtouris, Martin Luther King, Jr., and Bill Moyers. They are the forerunners, and the inspiration from their work illumines these pages.

I have profound gratitude for a host of partner-friends who have blessed my path. They include: Marc Porter – my partnering editor-in-chief who provided careful, insightful feedback and suggestions at every step along the way, and humor when I threatened to lose my way; Olivia Maynard – my founding partner in *The Wisdom Way*, who read the full manuscript with a marketer's and coach's eye, and has been an enduring source of affirmation and support; Melissa Cook – who many years ago saw the potential for a book in me long before anyone else, and who read the full manuscript and gave incredibly valuable suggestions; Bob Vitamonte – a fellow seeker on the path to innovative workplaces that call out the best in people, and who read the full manuscript and asked the difficult and necessary questions from a corporate perspective; Craig Schindler – with whom I have explored deep meaning and inspiring byways as we co-created *The Soul of Leadership* workshops; and Margo Wallace – who in many ways has been a wise mentor and an enthusiastic cheering squad, all rolled into one.

I'm also grateful to Professors Christine Downing, Randi Gray Kristensen, Dennis Slattery, David Miller, Kathleen Jenks, Dawn George, Hendrika de Vries, Patrick Mahaffey, Lionel Corbett, Ginette Paris, and Dan Noel, for all that I've learned studying with them, learning from them, and listening to their stories and sage advice. I was privileged to study at Pacifica Graduate Institute with a cohort of lively, inspiring, questing, and brilliant classmates with whom I have experienced true community. They include Janis Jennings, Patricia Brundage-Rude, Leigh Melander, Deanne Shartin, Corinne Cunningham, Martha Frankl, Brad Olsen, Shirley McNeil, Linda Shubert, Jeri Lynn Miller, Kay Todd, Christine Leigh, Darielle Richards, Rae Marie McReynolds, Beverly Black, Maren Hansen, David Grady, Joe Porter, Eileen Klatt, Jim MacLaren, and Jack Weiss.

If I have forgotten someone, it was certainly not by intention; know that even though your name may not appear in these pages, I hold your contribution with deep appreciation in my heart.

My deepest gratitude goes to my family; daughters Tanya and Alana, who have offered encouragement and their precious love, and Allen, my husband and partner in life, who has managed to both maintain his sanity and help me retain mine through a seemingly endless round of research, writing, and managing the myriad details involved in publishing—and for all he does to nurture and challenge and hold the high watch during difficult times for this beautiful planet we call home.

❧ About the Author ❧

Cynthia King is committed to peacemaking by improving communication between individuals and groups, transforming conflicts, and changing the ways people work together since her days as a Peace Corps Volunteer teaching nutrition and organizing women's groups in Honduras, Central America, in the early 1970s. Since that life-altering experience, she has been a dedicated global citizen, fascinated with the study of many different cultural and spiritual traditions and committed to co-creating soulful, meaningful partnerships based in authenticity, integrity, and wisdom. All of these themes have provided key threads in her work and research, and are woven throughout both this, her first book, and her forthcoming book, *The Feminine Face of Power: Finding Balance in a Divided World.*

Cynthia has over 25 years of experience as a communication and organizational development consultant, facilitator and trainer. She has consulted with a wide variety of government agencies, corporations, non-profit, and educational organizations around a variety of topics including:

- Interpersonal and intercultural communication
- Facilitating change and transitions
- Transforming conflicts: moving from *power-over* to *power-with* relationships
- Building collaborative teams and partnerships
- Building personal leadership capacity

Cynthia earned her Doctorate at Pacifica Graduate Institute in Mythology and Depth Psychology, with an emphasis in organizational applications. She holds an M.A. in Communication, with an emphasis in Intercultural Communication, and a B.A. in Spanish. Dr. King has taught communication courses at California State University, Chico, Feather River College, and Antioch University, Santa Barbara.

Cynthia lives with her husband Allen near Santa Barbara, California. She is the proud mother of two wonderful adult daughters.

❧ About the Contributing Editor ☙

 **Marc Porter,** editor, has been facilitating leadership programs, strategy sessions, and organizational development initiatives for over 20 years. He has managed academic business graduate programs and directed worldwide executive development for a non-profit organization. He holds a doctorate in Organizational Communication from Ohio University, where he also developed the earliest version of the Common Ground Model. His work has included examining the ethics of consulting and improving multicultural diversity and inclusion initiatives. Like Dr. Cynthia King, his approach to teaching, leading, and partnering is fundamentally maieutic. He lives in Northern California.

For more information about their speaking and consulting work, or to contact Dr. Cynthia King or Dr. Marc Porter, go to www.thewisdomway.com.

❧ Preview ☙

Cynthia King's next book, to be published in 2006, is *The Feminine Face of Power: Finding Balance in a Divided World.*

There is a deep wound that has been created by historic beliefs and systemic processes that rely on separation, prejudice, domination, and at times outright exclusion of all people, ideas, and things deemed "feminine," along with all minority groups who do not fit the prescribed, preferred, and dominant mold. That systemic prejudice and domination, which has prevented full citizen participation in many societies and organizations, has relied on an overriding, "masculine" face of power, and has contributed to ongoing cycles of attack, revenge, conflict, and war that keep the world—and many relationships—in an unbalanced and fragmented state.

There has been a growing awareness in the last several decades of the deep wounding that women particularly have sustained over the course of the past 5,000 years of the ascendancy of a system that values "masculine" over "feminine" and narrowly defines power as the opportunity to dominate and control others. Those narrow definitions and rigid structures have created a rift between the masculine and feminine aspects of our psyches and our culture.

This book provides an alternate view of power, beginning at the most intimate, intrapersonal level. This *Feminine Face of Power* incorporates the synergy that results from connection, inclusion, and accessing inner wisdom rather than limited and inadequate reliance on external knowing, separation, force, and control. This book is not an angry diatribe against men. Rather, it is a call for healing the wounds and bridging the gaps that have been created and sustained over the course of millennia. The healing process requires that both women and men seek to balance ways of knowing, ways of holding and sharing power, and ways of exploring our own inner depths while deepening and expanding our relationships.

The predominant archetype of the hero's journey is used to demonstrate the primary, external cycle of initiation and the impacts of the prevailing power paradigm. Myths and legends from a variety of cultures are called upon to illustrate the impacts of that mythic paradigm. The continuing journey of maturity is explored, beginning with a call for a secondary, inner cycle of initiation, wherein alternate archetypes come to the fore, as individuals and cultures re-balance the "masculine" and "feminine" aspects within themselves and come to realize the value and potential of transformed elders.

Watch for news of publication and ordering information at:

www.thewisdomway.com

Wisdom Way Press is an imprint of The Wisdom Way

The Wisdom Way is...

...a gathering of those yearning for a different way of being in the world—a way that:

- ➤ Taps into our deep inner knowing: our wisdom.
- ➤ Springs from ancient sources, connecting with those who have gone before and passing on the lore of wisdom traditions while translating applications for the modern world.
- ➤ Looks both inward for healing core wounds and "not enoughness" *and* outward, in the formation of communities of respect, trust, support, service, connection, harmony, and inclusion.
- ➤ Strengthens and sustains the spiritual practice of growing relationships wherein we bear witness to each other's stories, offer gentle guidance when we are troubled or confused, and celebrate our successes.
- ➤ Incorporates a spirituality that touches the deep yearning to experience wholeness and partnership in a fragmented, competitive and combative world.
- ➤ Consciously weaves various cultures' wisdom stories and teachings as the container for our personal, organizational, and social mythologies.

We have a wondrous gift available to each of us. The gift is called Wisdom. Welcome the Wonder!

For more information, check our website at:

www.thewisdomway.com

❧ Order Form ❧

☎ **Telephone Orders**: Call 1-877-228-5978 toll free. Have your credit
card ready.
▉ **email orders**: orders@thewisdomway.com
▣ **Postal Orders**: Wisdom Way Press, Cynthia King, P.O. Box 8913,
Santa Barbara, CA 93118   U.S.A.

Please send the following products: (I understand that I may return any
of them for a full refund—for any reason, no questions asked.)

_____

_____

Please send FREE information on:

q Speaking/seminars
q Organizational consulting
q Adding me to your mailing list

Name: _____

Address: _____

City: _____

State: _____ Zip: _____

Telephone: _____

Email address: _____

Sales tax: Add 7.75% for products shipped to California addresses.
Shipping by air:
U.S.: $4.50 for first book or disc, and $2.00 for each additional product.
International: $9.00 for first book or disk; $5.00 for each additional
product (estimate).

Payment: q Cheque   q Credit card:
q VISA q Master Card q AMEX q Discover q Optima

Card number: _____

Name on card: _____ Exp. Date: _____